# HIGH ALPINE CUISINE

# HIGH ALPINE CUISINE

Inspired Dishes from Extraordinary Mountain Escapes Around the World

✦

## MARLA MERIDITH

Founder of MarlaMeridith.com

PAGE STREET
PUBLISHING CO.

PAGE STREET
PUBLISHING CO.

Distributed by Macmillan, sales in Canada by The Canadian Manda Group.

22 21 20 19 18    1 2 3 4 5

ISBN-13: 978-1-62414-540-7

ISBN-10: 1-62414-540-x

Library of Congress Control Number: 2018934101

Cover and book design by Rosie Gutmann for Page Street Publishing Co.

Photography by Marla Meridith

Author photo by Abie Livesay

Printed and bound in China

For Leela and Lucas.
I love you to the moon,
back and beyond!

# Contents

# Introduction

I have a love affair with the mountains, and that's why I chose to move my family to the high country of Telluride, Colorado, five years ago. We live nearly 10,000 feet (3 km) in the sky. The air is thinner up here, and the skies are the bluest I've ever seen. It's the closest I've ever gotten to heaven on earth, and it's a far cry from my childhood years growing up on Long Island, New York, and living for thirteen years in Orange County, California (the OC). I craved a place so different than the others I had lived in. I wanted the great outdoors to reign supreme and for nature to be the center of my world. The mountains never lie; they are imposing, powerful and they always put you in your place.

I launched my blog, FamilyFreshCooking.com, back in 2009. The focus was on the meals I cooked daily for my family. My kids were just three and six at the time, and we were living in the OC. I knew back then (and way before) that something big was missing from my life—I knew what it was, but I had to find a way to get us here. To the mountains.

Most of our family vacations were spent here in Telluride. When not in Telli, I would pine for the high pistes, cool air and spectacular views. The mountains were calling to me no matter where I was. In 2012, we moved here full time, which was long overdue and greatly celebrated! Telluride is like a dream come true, an outdoor wonderland for kids, adults and pets. And do we have pets in the mountains: here they outnumber their humans two to one!

With the move I also changed my blog name to my name, MarlaMeridith.com. It made more sense for me to have a space where I could share all kinds of lifestyle posts. From travel to fashion, skiing and beauty tips, I wanted to share my voice openly and authentically without any restraints from my blog name. The main focus on my blog is still my creative, family-friendly recipes, but with all the other fun stuff, too! My blog allows me to welcome each day with a renewed creative spirit and the chance to be your culinary and lifestyle inspiration.

# How Alpine Cuisine Speaks to Me

High country food is honest, bold and completely delicious. It's meant to tempt the palate and nourish the soul no matter what the season. There's a starkness in the mountains, an isolating quality that is softened with utterly tempting homemade meals. Mountain food is not fancy, but it's completely seductive in its own way.

My love for honest, simple food was sparked when I was a kid. At that time, my family and I would travel a few times a year to Devon, in the English countryside. My aunt and uncle had an organic dairy farm, and it was there that I would settle into another culture, especially during long summers, and taste all the offerings from the farm: milk straight from the dairy, farmhouse cheeses, cured meats like I had never had before, the freshest fruits and veggies. It's where we picked blackberries from the bushes, each bursting with sun-ripened flavor. This is where my palate was born. It was a gift that keeps giving back to my life every single day.

I'm also a fan of the four seasons. They each offer so much in their uniqueness, especially in the mountains. Seasons control the foods we eat, the fashions we wear and the activities we love to do. It's these constant changes that thrill and exhilarate me. I always love watching how excited people get with the change of seasonal ingredients.

And finally, my cooking is influenced by my love of the mountains. My first trip to the Swiss Alps was about seven years ago, and now I'm completely hooked. The mountain chalets and huts have some of the best food, drinks and views I've ever experienced. I'll never forget my first experience ordering raclette (page 65) at Chez Vrony while overlooking the Matterhorn in Zermatt. Flavors taste even more pronounced when looking at such beauty. Whether in Aspen, Crested Butte or Telluride, Colorado, or in the Italian, Austrian or French Alps, mountain meals are meant to be sturdy, and the flavors never disappoint. Cheeses, cured meats, potatoes and strudels are just some of the hearty foods you encounter. It's this high alpine cuisine that has become a favorite of mine. It is through food and drink that I have enjoyed my most profound experiences with others. Food is a celebration of life.

In the pages of this cookbook, my job is to be your on- and off-piste culinary tour guide. I want you to experience the places I have been through beautiful flavors. I've been to many ski resorts around the world, and those are the ones highlighted in this cookbook. There are many more locations on my bucket list. I have a never-ending pursuit of alpine wonders. If you have traveled to these places, I hope to spark your memories, too. No matter what your favorite mountain is to frolic on and no matter what part of the world, I want you to be able to taste that mountain vacation and remember how wonderful it was. And if you have little connection with the high country, I can guarantee you that alpine cooking will speak as much to your taste buds as it does to your inner soul.

All of my favorite recipes from these places are made extra delicious for you in this cookbook. I took such great joy in developing, tasting, testing, styling and photographing each and every one of them. Mountain recipes are often classics and are passed down from generation to generation. I enjoyed applying my modern tweaks and twists to the traditional ones and coming up with brand-new ideas as well.

All of my recipes are easy enough for the beginner cook, but tempting enough for any level. Some recipes take a bit more time than others, but I promise any extra time is well spent. Try to be patient and let the ingredients do their thing. The nice thing about a lot of alpine cooking is its slow food style. Each step of the process is meant to be savored and enjoyed, from the first lick of a flame to the first bite.

The ingredients I use throughout this book can be found at most markets. You may occasionally wish to place an online order if you desire the utmost in authenticity, but that is certainly not required. I've designed this cookbook with easily obtainable ingredients in mind. I want you to have a cookbook that you know you can rely on for a lifetime and beyond, with recipes to share with loved ones, family and friends. I dream of the edges of these pages getting tattered as you make these recipes again and again. Always feel free to make changes along the way. Cooking is your canvas, too.

## Equipment and Ingredients

A few items you will want to have on hand are cast-iron skillets in a few sizes and a fondue pot.

Cast-iron skillets have become my everything in the kitchen! I use a few sizes throughout this book, my favorites being a 10- and a 12-inch (25- and 30-cm) skillet. Quality comes at a low price point, which makes it easy to have a few. These skillets are excellent heat conductors, and I love the fact that they can go from stove top to oven to table. Also make sure you have some good oven mitts at the ready to handle these skillets. The handles get extremely hot! Investing in a good fondue pot is great for entertaining and family meals, too.

Always buy the best ingredients you can find at prices you can afford. I try to purchase locally grown ingredients when available, which can be tricky living at this altitude! In these recipes I advise what the best ingredients are to make the most authentically delicious dishes. When it comes to things like butter, cheese and milk, I typically go with the full-fat versions, not fat-free. For ingredients like maple syrup and vanilla extract, I purchase the purest forms without additives, and it makes a difference in the overall flavor and quality of the dish.

The recipes in this book are suitable for all altitudes, whether you live by the sea or up high in the sky. There are no special adjustments that need to be made for either.

I hope these dishes will encourage you to dream about your next great adventure. Whether you love the high country or not, I'm certain these recipes will win your heart.

# Belly-Filling Breakfasts

---◆---

Days in the mountains are usually spent doing something active outdoors no matter what the season. Alarms go off early to get first tracks on powder days in the winter. In the summer there's a race to be the first one to the river for fly fishing. Summer also means monsoon season, so to stay dry, outdoor activities need to be done by 3 p.m. or earlier. A hearty breakfast is always in great demand. Whether sweet or savory, there's something for everyone. I'm always excited to see what the offerings will be in high alpine huts, campfire wake-ups, five-star brunches and early-morning hikes with friends. Breakfast is not to be missed when you have an up-and-down vertical to tackle.

# Alpine Strawberries and Mascarpone Stuffed French Toast

4 slices country bread (brioche, challah, potato), each cut at least 1 inch (2.5 cm) thick

## Strawberry filling

6 large fresh strawberries, sliced

1 tbsp (14 g) light brown sugar

4 oz (114 g) mascarpone cheese, room temperature

½ tsp pure vanilla extract

1 tsp lemon zest

2 tbsp (30 ml) pure maple syrup

Pinch of salt

## Egg dip

4 large eggs

½ tsp pure vanilla extract

¼ tsp salt

## Cooking and serving

1 tbsp (14 g) unsalted butter

Powdered sugar

Maple syrup

Softened butter

Remaining sugared strawberries

As much as I adore staying at grandiose five-star mountain properties, I also have a thing for dainty country inns and cozy bed and breakfasts. During my first trip to Telluride back in 2003, we stayed in town at the San Sophia Inn, which was known for its amazing belly-filling breakfasts. Sadly, the B&B is no longer here, but the memories of the breakfasts are surely not forgotten by all those who visited there. This stuffed French toast is reminiscent of the kinds of sweet treats we would indulge in before hitting the slopes.

*Serves 4*

With a serrated knife, cut a deep pocket into one edge of each slice of bread. Cut as far through as you can to create a large enough envelope for the filling.

To make the filling, combine sliced strawberries with the brown sugar in a small bowl. Let sit for 5 minutes to release some juices. In another bowl, with a wooden spoon, combine the mascarpone, vanilla, lemon zest, maple syrup and salt. Add half of the strawberries to the mix. Combine well, pressing the berries against the sides of the bowl to release some juices.

With a small spoon, carefully stuff the mascarpone mixture into the bread envelopes. You will use about one-quarter of the mix per sandwich.

To make the egg dip, whisk the eggs with the vanilla and salt in a clean bowl.

Heat the butter in a 12-inch (30-cm) cast-iron skillet over medium heat. Using clean hands, dip one stuffed French toast into the egg mixture. Flip to make sure all sides are evenly coated. Let the excess drip off. Continue for the rest of the French toast. Immediately place each piece of egg-dipped bread into the buttered skillet. Fit as many as you can in the pan, with some space in between to flip. Cook for about 3 to 4 minutes on each side until you have a golden crust and eggs are cooked.

Dust with powdered sugar, and serve immediately, with toppings on the side.

# Cinnamon Applesauce Muffins with Streusel Topping

## Cinnamon streusel topping

¼ cup (31 g) all-purpose flour

2 tbsp (28 g) light brown sugar

1 tsp ground cinnamon

Pinch of salt

2 tbsp (28 g) unsalted butter, softened

## Muffins

2 cups (250 g) all-purpose flour

½ cup (100 g) granulated sugar

1 tsp ground cinnamon

2 tsp (10 g) baking powder

¼ tsp salt

1 large egg

½ cup (114 g) unsalted butter, melted

1 cup (252 g) unsweetened applesauce

1 tsp pure vanilla extract

I love spending time at Element 52 here in Telluride; it's a chic, cozy slope-side property where a lot of my good friends live. As soon as I walk into the living room in the morning, there's coffee brewing, a fire roaring and freshly baked cinnamon muffins ready to go. There's nothing like a warm muffin (or a few!) to wake you up and get you kick-started for a busy day ahead. My muffin recipe will fill your home with the gorgeous smell of cinnamon sugar. Make extra streusel if you just can't get enough.

*Makes 12 muffins*

Preheat the oven to 375°F (190°C) with the rack in the middle. Grease or prepare a standard-size muffin tray with liners.

To make the streusel topping, whisk together the dry ingredients and cut in the butter until you have a crumbly texture.

To make the muffins, whisk together the dry ingredients in a large bowl. In another bowl, combine the wet ingredients in a large bowl. Add the wet to the dry and combine into a smooth batter. Spoon the batter into the muffin cups, about three-fourths full. Top each muffin equally with the streusel topping.

Bake for 18 to 20 minutes, or until a toothpick comes out virtually crumb-free. Let them cool a few minutes before serving.

# Wild Chanterelle Scrambled Eggs with Goat Cheese and Fresh Herbs

## Mushrooms

2 tbsp (30 ml) olive oil

1 tbsp (14 g) unsalted butter

½ cup (75 g) finely chopped leeks, white part only

1 clove garlic, minced

2 cups (110 g) chanterelle mushrooms, sliced if on the larger side

Salt and pepper to taste

## Eggs

1 tbsp (14 g) unsalted butter

1 tbsp (15 ml) olive oil

4 eggs

Splash of water

2 oz (56 g) goat cheese

1 tsp chopped fresh thyme

1 tsp chopped fresh rosemary

2–4 slices thick-cut rustic bread

Goat cheese crumbles and fresh herbs for serving

I have never seen or tasted eggs as golden and delicious as the ones I enjoyed fresh off the farm in the Alps. With the simple addition of cracked pepper and some salt, they are like nothing else—rich, decadent and pure. But when you do crave a little something more, try this recipe with fresh herbs and goat cheese. They are beautiful paired with eggs. Add the golden, buttery hue and aromatic flavor of wild chanterelle mushrooms and you've got quite the gourmet feast. Serve on a rustic slice of crusty bread.

*Serves 2–3*

To prepare the mushrooms, heat the oil and melt the butter in a 10-inch (25-cm) cast-iron skillet over medium heat. Add the leeks and garlic. Cook until fragrant, about 2 minutes. Add the chanterelles and cook until softened, about 4 minutes. Transfer to a bowl. Season with salt and pepper.

To prepare the eggs, melt the butter and olive oil over medium heat into the same skillet (do not clean it). In a bowl, whisk the eggs with a splash of water. Pour into the skillet, and combine well with a soft spatula until the eggs are firm.

Crumble the goat cheese over the top, and fold it in with the thyme and rosemary until well combined and warmed, 2 minutes.

Place the eggs onto a slice of toasted bread, and top with the chanterelles, goat cheese and herbs.

# Cast-Iron Skillet Cinnamon Rolls with Maple Pumpkin Cream Cheese Frosting

### Sweet roll dough

3½ cups (437 g) unbleached all-purpose flour

1 (¼-oz [7-g]) package active dry yeast

½ cup (120 ml) whole milk

½ cup (115 g) sour cream

6 tbsp (85 g) unsalted butter, cut into cubes

⅓ cup (60 g) granulated sugar

2 tsp (12 g) salt

1 large egg, lightly beaten

### Filling

¾ cup (150 g) light brown sugar, firmly packed

2 tbsp (16 g) ground cinnamon

½ cup (114 g) unsalted butter, melted

### Frosting

12 oz (340 g) cream cheese, at room temperature

½ cup (114 g) unsalted butter, at room temperature

⅓ cup (82 g) unsweetened pumpkin purée (not pie filling)

1–2 cups (125–250 g) powdered sugar, sifted (sweeten to taste)

¼ cup (80 g) pure maple syrup

1 tsp pumpkin pie spice

½ cup (65 g) toasted walnuts or pecans, optional

If you have ever experienced the mountains, then you have likely experienced feeling breathless and well exercised. The great news is you might have also experienced losing weight no matter what you eat. My friends and I always joke about how much more we can eat and stay thin living at this altitude. Thank goodness for that—it makes diving into these crazy-good cinnamon rolls all the more fun!

*Serves 10*

To make the dough, combine the flour and yeast in the bowl of a stand mixer. Heat the milk, sour cream, butter, granulated sugar and salt in a medium saucepan over medium heat. Stir occasionally, until just warm, 3 minutes; you do not want it to simmer or boil. Add the milk mixture to the mixer bowl with the flour. Beat with the paddle attachment. Add the egg and beat until a dough forms. Beat for a few minutes until the dough pulls away from the edges of the bowl.

Remove the dough from the mixer bowl with lightly floured hands and place in a large oiled bowl to rise. Cover and let rise in a warm room until the dough has a chance to double in size. This will take about 90 minutes, depending on the temperature of the room. It may take a bit longer if the room is not so warm.

To make the filling, whisk together the brown sugar and cinnamon in a bowl. Coat a 10-inch (25-cm) cast-iron skillet with vegetable oil or cooking spray. Preheat the oven to 350°F (180°C) with the rack in the middle.

Once the dough has risen, on a lightly floured surface, roll the dough out to a roughly 14 x 10-inch (35.5 x 25-cm) rectangle. Brush the dough with some of the melted butter. Make sure to coat the entire rectangle. Sprinkle the cinnamon sugar mixture evenly over the top.

Start to roll the dough from the long edge away from you. Continue to roll until you have a log. Seal the edge with some melted butter. Cut the log until you have about ten 1-inch (2.5-cm)-tall slices. Place the slices into the prepared skillet. Drizzle any remaining butter over the top of the rolls.

Bake for 30 minutes uncovered, until the cinnamon rolls are golden brown. Remove from the oven and let cool before adding the frosting.

While the rolls are baking, make the frosting. With the paddle attachment, beat the cream cheese, butter and pumpkin together on medium speed until smooth. Add the powdered sugar, maple syrup and pumpkin pie spice, and beat on low until just combined; increase to medium speed until you have a smooth consistency.

Slather the frosting on top of the cooled cinnamon rolls and serve. Top with nuts, if desired.

# Overnight Banana Nut Bircher Muesli

2 cups (180 g) old-fashioned rolled oats

1½ cups (350 ml) milk (any kind is good; I use 1%)

½ cup (123 g) plain Greek yogurt

1 ripe, mashed banana

¼ cup (27 g) slivered, toasted almonds

⅓ cup (50 g) raisins

2 tbsp (30 ml) pure maple syrup

2 tbsp (28 g) chia seeds

2 tsp (10 ml) fresh lemon juice

Splash of pure vanilla extract

Waking up in the Alps is a glorious experience, but even more exciting is dashing down to breakfast. Every hotel, inn and family home has a favorite version of this healthy breakfast staple. You can add endless flavors, seasonings and fruits. You can serve it warm or cold. The one real constant is whole-grain oats and a soaking liquid (the liquid can also be varied). The extra bonus with this recipe is that you can make it the night before you need it—perfect for those busy mornings when you need to get out the door. Pack it in a mason jar if you're having brekkie on the go.

*Serves 4*

Add all of the ingredients to a large bowl and combine well. Let sit in the refrigerator for at least 30 minutes or as long as overnight. This recipe has the creamiest texture if you let it sit overnight before serving.

# Lemon-Ricotta Blintzes with Mountain Berries Sauce

## Blintzes

1 cup (240 ml) whole milk

1 cup (125 g) all-purpose flour

¼ cup (57 g) unsalted butter, melted

3 large eggs

Pinch of kosher salt

1 tbsp (14 g) granulated sugar

1 tsp pure vanilla extract

## Lemon-ricotta filling

8 oz (230 g) ricotta cheese

8 oz (230 g) cream cheese

2 tbsp (30 g) powdered sugar

2 tsp (4 g) lemon zest

1 tbsp (15 ml) fresh lemon juice

## Berry compote

12 oz (2 pints [336 g]) blueberries

6 oz (1 pint [168 g]) blackberries

6 oz (1 pint [168 g]) raspberries

¼ cup (60 ml) pure maple syrup

2 tsp (10 ml) fresh lemon juice

¼ cup (60 ml) water

Blintzes are a hearty and delicious mountain breakfast. You can make the crepes ahead of time, wrap snugly and freeze until ready to use. You can prep them a month before you need them, which is nice for camping and cold winter morning wake-ups. Use your favorite berries in the compote. If you have any extra berry sauce you might want to use it on ice cream too!

*Makes 10 blintzes*

To make the blintzes, add all of the ingredients to a large bowl and whisk together by hand or in a mixer until well combined. Cover and place in the fridge for at least 1 hour or up to 12.

Lightly oil and heat a nonstick skillet over medium heat. Place ¼ cup (60 ml) of the batter into the pan. With the back of a spoon, swirl the batter until you have about a 6-inch (15-cm) crepe. Cook for about 1 to 1½ minutes, or until the crepe is lightly browned. Gently flip the crepe and cook for about 1 more minute. Place in a stack until ready to use. Refrigerate if not using immediately.

To make the filling, mix all of the ingredients in a bowl until well combined.

To make the berry compote, combine all of the ingredients in a saucepan over medium-high heat. Bring to a boil, then simmer for about 7 minutes; the berries will soften and the sauce will thicken a bit. Mash them against the sides of the pan with the back of a wooden spoon. Let the sauce cool 30 minutes; it will thicken as it cools.

Preheat the oven to 375°F (190°C). Heat a cast-iron skillet with some butter over medium heat. Place 3 to 4 tablespoons (23 to 30 g) of the ricotta filling into the center of the crepe. Fold the tops down and the sides over, so you have an envelope. Gently place the blintzes onto the skillet. Cook for 1 to 2 minutes on each side until the blintzes are golden brown. Continue this for all of the blintzes. Add more butter to the pan as needed. Place the cooked blintzes in a casserole dish. Bake for 12 minutes, until the blintzes are hot and the cheese filling is soft. Serve immediately with the berry compote.

# High Country Wild Blueberry Buckle Coffee Cake with Streusel Topping

## Streusel topping

⅓ cup (67 g) sugar

½ cup (62 g) all-purpose flour

1 tsp ground cinnamon

⅛ tsp salt

¼ cup (57 g) unsalted butter, cold cut into ¼-inch (6-mm) pieces

¼ cup (30 g) walnuts, chopped small

## Cake

2 cups (250 g) all-purpose flour

2 tsp (10 g) baking powder

½ tsp salt

¾ cup (150 g) sugar

4 tbsp (57 g) unsalted butter, softened

1 large egg

1 tsp pure vanilla extract

½ cup (120 ml) milk

2 cups (280 g) fresh or frozen wild blueberries

There's nothing like playing hard in the mountains and sleeping like a baby at night. I get the best rest after a full day outdoors. Waking up to an epic breakfast is a bonus too. I love my sweets and savories, usually on one plate. It's lovely to have a coffee cake at the ready for family and house guests. Waking up to the smell of piping hot blueberries and streusel will get you jumping out of bed and ready for another day of outdoor fun. Streusel lovers, there's a nice hearty layer on this cake. Double the portion if you think you might want even more!

*Serves 12–16*

Preheat the oven to 375°F (190°C). Lightly grease a 9 x 9 x 2-inch (23 x 23 x 5-cm) square pan with cooking spray or butter.

To make the topping, whisk together the sugar, flour, cinnamon and salt in a bowl. Mix in the butter; I use my fingers and gently press the butter into the flour mixture. You want to form a crumble. Add the nuts, and combine them into the mix.

To make the cake, whisk together the flour, baking powder and salt in another bowl.

In the bowl of a stand mixer, beat the sugar, butter, egg and vanilla together until well combined. Slowly add the milk and flour in alternating additions, ending with the flour. Mix with a spatula or spoon until well combined. Add the blueberries and gently fold them into the mix.

Pour the batter into the prepared pan. Sprinkle the streusel topping over the batter, being sure to cover the entire surface evenly.

Bake the cake for 40 to 45 minutes or until a knife or skewer comes out virtually crumb-free. Place the cake on a rack to cool for about 10 minutes. You can cut slices directly from the pan, or carefully remove it to serve. The cake will release easily from the pan if you run a knife around the edges first.

# Crisp Rösti with Smoked Salmon, Crème Fraîche and Chives (Swiss Hash Browns)

### Rösti

2 or 3 russet or Yukon Gold potatoes, peeled

1 tsp salt

½ tsp ground black pepper

2 tbsp (28 g) unsalted butter, divided

2 tbsp (30 ml) olive oil, divided

2 cloves garlic, smashed and minced

### Toppings

3–4 oz (85–114 g) crème fraîche

4 oz (114 g) smoked salmon

2 tbsp (7 g) freshly chopped chives

Salt and pepper

This Swiss-style savory shredded potato cake is mouthwatering and is not to be missed. I had my first experience with rösti at a restaurant called Hauser in St. Moritz. I will never forget enjoying every single bite. There are many toppings you can put on rösti—the sky's the limit. One thing is standard, though: the base is always a crispy bed of hash brown–style potatoes. Serve for breakfast, brunch, après or any time of the day!

*Serves 2*

To make the rösti, parboil the potatoes in salted water until just tender, but not soft, 5 minutes. Let the potatoes cool and chill for at least a couple of hours. Grate the potatoes with the big holes of a cheese grater. Place the grated potatoes in some paper towels and gently press to squeeze out any excess water. Season the potatoes with the salt and pepper.

Heat half of the butter and half of the olive oil in a 12-inch (30-cm) cast-iron skillet over medium heat. When it's sizzling, add the potato mixture and garlic. Spread them around the pan so they are in a single layer. You want to be sure they are spread out so they have enough space to crisp up properly.

Cook the mixture for 5 minutes, letting the bottom brown, and gently press into the cake with the bottom of a spatula. Shake the pan a bit to loosen the potatoes; cook another 10 minutes while watching so the potatoes don't burn.

Carefully flip the potatoes onto a plate (it's OK if they break up a bit; you can always reshape them later), and add the rest of the butter and oil to the pan. Swirl it around so it's well coated. Flip the potatoes back into the skillet so the uncooked side is down. Cook for another 10 minutes or until golden brown and crispy.

Divide the rösti into two pieces and plate, gently pressing back into a cake shape. Top each with crème fraîche, smoked salmon and chives. Season with salt and pepper. Serve immediately.

# Silver-Dollar Buttermilk Pancakes with Maple Bourbon Butter Sauce

### Pancakes

1½ cups (187 g) unbleached all-purpose flour

½ tsp baking soda

¾ tsp fine salt

3 tbsp (44 ml) pure maple syrup

2 large eggs

1½ cups plus 3 tbsp (400 ml) buttermilk

3 tbsp (43 g) unsalted butter, melted and cooled, plus more for skillet

1 tsp pure vanilla extract

### Sauce

2 tbsp (30 ml) bourbon

1 cup (240 ml) pure maple syrup

3 tbsp (44 g) unsalted butter

Salt to taste

This hearty breakfast will tempt pancake lovers beyond their wildest dreams. The maple bourbon sauce is totally addictive and is great on ice cream too. Cooked up in a sizzling cast-iron skillet, this breakfast can easily be made in your home, on ski hut trips or even camping. Who says you have to skip a glamorous breakfast even when out on the trail? Not I, ever.

*Serves 4–6*

To make the pancakes, whisk together the flour, baking soda and salt in a medium bowl. In another bowl mix together the maple syrup, eggs, buttermilk, butter and vanilla. Add the wet mixture into the dry and combine well, but do not over mix. Leave out at room temperature for 30 minutes.

While the batter is sitting, make the sauce. In a small skillet, heat the sauce ingredients over medium heat. Mix well. Once the butter has melted and the sauce is well combined, season with some salt to taste. Remove from the heat and set aside.

Heat a 12-inch (30-cm) cast-iron skillet over medium heat with a generous pat of butter. When the butter starts to sizzle, add 2-tablespoon (30-ml) portions of the batter to the pan. Leave some room in between the pancakes so you can flip them easily. Once you see bubbles start to form on the tops of the pancakes, about a minute, it's time to flip them. Flip and cook another minute or until both sides are golden brown. Continue to make pancakes until you have used up all the batter, adding butter as needed to the skillet.

Plate the pancakes and serve immediately with the sauce on the side.

# Strawberry Lavender Granola

½ cup (100 g) quartered strawberries (fresh or frozen)

½ cup (118 ml) honey

3 tbsp (45 ml) coconut oil, melted

½ tsp kosher salt

1 tsp pure vanilla extract

1 tbsp (6 g) culinary lavender, finely ground

3 cups (270 g) old-fashioned rolled oats (don't use instant oats)

½ cup (65 g) walnuts or pecans, chopped small

½ cup (95 g) dried strawberries, chopped

Granola is a healthy, energy-packed food that I love for breakfast. It's great with milk or yogurt. It's perfect for on-the-go snacking or on travel days too. Ruby-red alpine strawberries and various hues of lavender can be found decorating the hilltops in the summer months. It's always a treat to see a tiny strawberry right by your feet when hiking—a surprising and juicy treat! The flavors in this granola bring sunshine into the stormiest of days.

*Serves 8*

Preheat the oven to 325°F (165°C). Spray a baking sheet with cooking spray.

In a saucepan, combine the strawberries, honey, coconut oil, salt, vanilla and lavender. Heat over medium-low heat, mix to combine. Bring to a simmer for 3 minutes. Transfer the mixture to a blender and mix into a smooth sauce.

Combine this mixture with the oats and nuts, making sure the oats are evenly coated. Spread evenly onto a baking sheet. Bake for 20 to 25 minutes or until the granola is golden brown. Mix every 5 to 7 minutes to ensure even cooking. Remove from the oven and let cool. Mix in the dried strawberries.

The granola will harden as it cools. Store in an airtight container for up to a week.

# Trail Mix Scones

1½ cups (187 g) unbleached all-purpose flour

1 cup (90 g) old-fashioned rolled oats (don't use instant oats)

¼ cup plus 1 tbsp (64 g) granulated sugar

2½ tsp (12 g) baking powder

½ tsp baking soda

½ tsp fine salt

¾ cup (170 g) unsalted butter, chilled and cut into small pieces

4 oz (114 g) cream cheese, chilled

½ cup (123 g) Greek yogurt

1 large egg, lightly beaten

½ cup (75 g) chopped, pitted dates tossed in flour to coat

½ cup (88 g) semisweet chocolate chips

½ cup (65 g) pecans, walnuts or peanuts

¼ cup (36 g) dried cranberries

¼ cup (40 g) golden raisins

2 tbsp (30 ml) heavy cream or milk

Coarse sugar for sprinkling on top

I'm so in love with scones. I like how quickly and easily they come together, how amazing they taste and the joyful fact that I can toss a few in my Louis Vuitton tote or ski backpack. My Trail Mix Scones bring together the fun of crumbly, lightly sweetened scones with your favorite trail mix ingredients. Have fun with these, and I urge you to get creative with the add-ins.

*Makes 12 scones*

Preheat the oven to 400°F (205°C) with the rack in the middle. Line a baking sheet with parchment paper or spray with cooking oil.

In a food processor, blend the flour, oats, granulated sugar, baking powder, baking soda and salt together until the oats are coarsely ground. Add the butter and cream cheese, and pulse until a coarse meal forms. Add the yogurt and egg. Pulse until everything is just mixed together. Do not over mix.

Transfer the dough to a lightly floured work surface. Knead in the dates, chocolate chips, nuts, cranberries and raisins with as few turns as possible. Pat the dough into two discs about ½ inch (1.3 cm) thick. With a sharp knife or pizza cutter, cut the dough into 12 wedges and place on the prepared baking sheet. Brush the tops of the dough wedges with the cream. Sprinkle some coarse sugar over the tops.

Bake until golden brown, about 16 to 18 minutes. Serve warm or at room temperature. Enjoy within a few days. Store in an airtight container at room temperature.

# Freshies:
# Salads and Veggies

———— ♦ ————

We refer to first tracks on powder ski runs as getting some "freshies." This is the ultimate alpine experience for any downhill skier; you feel like you are floating on a cloud! In this cookbook, freshies are recipes that require minimal cooking, the freshest ingredients and a whole lot of flavor. Gathering fresh produce is a special time in the mountains that we never take for granted. It's only for a few short months in the summer. We thoroughly enjoy the abundance when it's available to us.

# Erdäpfelsalat
# (Austrian Potato Salad)

2 lb (1 kg) Yukon Gold or other waxy potatoes, peeled

Kosher salt

3 tbsp (45 ml) white wine vinegar

½ cup (120 ml) low-sodium vegetable broth

¼ cup (60 ml) vegetable oil

1 tbsp (15 g) Dijon mustard

¾ cup (90 g) minced red onion

2 tbsp (7 g) minced fresh chives

1 tsp sugar

½ tsp salt

Pepper to taste

Garnish with more chives and chive blossoms

Believe it or not, potato salad can taste fresh, light and not gloppy. There is no mayonnaise in this salad. The Austrians nailed excellent flavor with their vinegar- and broth-based dressing. I've enjoyed this potato salad as a side to so many dishes in Austria and Switzerland. It's the perfect accompaniment to meat and veggie dishes.

*Serves 4*

Bring the potatoes to a boil with well-salted water. Simmer for 15 to 20 minutes or until fork tender. Drain the potatoes and let them cool so you can handle them. When cool to the touch, cut into small, bite-size pieces.

With a soft spatula, toss the potatoes with the rest of the ingredients. Make sure they are all well coated. Taste and adjust any ingredients if desired. Let sit at room temperature for a few hours to allow the sauce to soak into the potatoes. If over 4 hours, cover and chill in the fridge.

This salad is even better when prepared the day before you want to eat it. Serve with garnishes, chilled or at room temperature.

# Bündnerfleisch Salad with Swiss-French Salad Dressing

Dressing

½ tsp fine salt

½ tsp finely ground black pepper

½ tsp garlic powder

2 tsp (10 g) brown mustard

6 oz (168 ml) olive oil

3 tbsp (45 ml) white or cider vinegar

1 large egg or 2 tbsp (30 ml) heavy cream

1 tsp sugar

A few tablespoons of veggie broth or water

Salad

6 heaping cups (215 g) fresh salad greens

1 bunch skinny asparagus

1 bell pepper, sliced into thin strips

2 oz (56 g) Gruyère or Appenzeller cheese, thinly sliced

Any other veggies you love!

6 oz (168 g) Bündnerfleisch

Bündnerfleisch, or Viande des Grisons, is a delicious air-dried meat that is produced in the canton of Graubünden, Switzerland. You will see it used in many savory high alpine dishes. This salad really shows off its flavor with fresh veggies and a traditional Swiss salad dressing. Serve as an appetizer, main dish or side dish.

*Serves 2–4*

To make the dressing, combine all of the ingredients, leaving out the broth or water, in a blender. Blend until pale in color. Add in the broth or water until it thins out just a bit. Store in an airtight jar in the refrigerator up to 4 days.

To make the salad, divide the salad ingredients among the plates and drizzle the dressing over the top. Serve with extra dressing on the side.

# Cast-Iron Skillet Ratatouille

Ratatouille

2 zucchini

2 yellow squash

2 small eggplants

5 plum tomatoes

1 red onion

Sauce

3 tbsp (45 ml) olive oil

1 medium yellow onion, diced (about 1 cup [150 g])

2 cloves garlic, minced

½ yellow bell pepper, chopped

½ red bell pepper, chopped

1 (28-oz [795-g]) jar of diced tomatoes

2 tbsp (5 g) chopped fresh parsley

2 tbsp (5 g) chopped fresh basil

1 tsp kosher salt

½ tsp ground black pepper

There's nothing like rolling into a warming hut and being greeted with the smell of garlic and roasted veggies. It gets your hunger on big time! This ratatouille casserole is super nurturing on the coldest of days. It feeds a large group of people, and it offers up plenty of leftovers. Serve with a side of rice or quinoa. Ratatouille is a traditional French dish that you can find all over the Alps. This veggie coin styling is a pretty way to present this tasty dish. Serve at your next dinner party—a great option for vegans as well.

*Serves 8*

Preheat the oven to 375°F (190°C).

To make the ratatouille, slice the zucchini, squash, eggplant, tomatoes and onion into ¼-inch (6-mm) coins.

To make the sauce, heat the oil in a 12-inch (30-cm) cast-iron skillet over medium heat. Sauté the onion for 5 minutes, and add the garlic and peppers. Sauté for another 5 minutes, stirring during cooking. Add the jarred tomatoes and bring to a simmer for 5 minutes. Stir in the parsley, basil, salt and pepper. Taste the sauce to see if you want to make any seasoning adjustments. Carefully transfer the sauce to a blender and puree until well combined.

Pour three-fourths of the sauce back into the same skillet. Place the veggie coins in a circle and repeat the pattern until you have filled the pan. You might need to trim some of the veggies more to fit them in a pretty pattern. Cover the veggies with the last quarter of sauce.

Cover the skillet with foil and bake for 45 minutes. Remove the foil and bake for another 15 minutes until the veggies are soft.

# High Country Salad with Butternut Squash and Apple Cider Vinaigrette

## Butternut squash

1 large butternut squash (5–6 cups [625–750 g] cubed)

¼ cup (60 ml) grapeseed oil

3 tbsp (45 ml) pure maple syrup

1 tbsp (7 g) ground cinnamon

½ tsp salt

## Apple cider vinaigrette

½ cup (120 ml) canola oil

¼ cup (60 ml) apple cider

¼ cup (60 ml) apple cider vinegar

¼ tsp garlic powder

1 tbsp (15 g) Dijon mustard

¼ tsp salt

¼ tsp black pepper

2 tbsp diced shallots

## Salad

1 bunch of kale (5–6 cups [335–402 g]), ribs removed, use leafy parts only

⅓ cup (50 g) vinaigrette or to taste

1 cup (190 g) cooked quinoa

1 Honeycrisp apple (or your favorite apple variety), diced

½ cup (75 g) pomegranate seeds

½ cup (65 g) toasted pecans, chopped

⅓ cup (33 g) red onion, sliced

¼ cup (60 g) crumbled goat cheese

Hearty winter squash is always a welcomed addition to any mountain meal. This salad captures all the delicious flavors of fall and winter. My roasted maple cinnamon butternut squash is irresistible—it's almost hard not to eat it all in one serving! This salad is great as a first course, main or side dish.

*Serves 4*

To make the squash, pierce several holes in the squash with a sharp knife or fork. Microwave for 5 to 6 minutes until the skin is soft enough to cut. Let cool a bit so you can handle the squash. Cut in half and remove the seeds; you can roast these or discard. Trim off the skin and cut the flesh into 1-inch (2.5-cm) cubes.

Preheat the oven to 425°F (220°C) with the rack in the middle. Prepare a baking sheet with tin foil; this will make cleanup much easier.

In a bowl, whisk together the oil, maple syrup, cinnamon and salt. Place the squash on the baking sheet in a single layer. Drizzle the maple mixture over the squash. Toss with clean hands, making sure every piece is well coated. Bake for 30 minutes, rotating the pan and tossing the squash with tongs halfway through cooking.

To make the dressing, place all of the ingredients in a glass jar fitted with a lid. Shake well. Makes 1 cup (240 ml) of dressing.

In a large bowl, toss the kale with the dressing. I like to mix it well with clean hands to make sure the kale is completely coated. Add the quinoa into the kale and combine well.

Place in a serving bowl and top with the squash, apple, pomegranate seeds, pecans, onion and goat cheese. Adjust any ingredients to taste. Serve immediately with additional dressing on the side.

# Nüsslisalat with Tarragon Vinaigrette

8 slices bacon

6 slices white bread

5 oz (140 g) Mâche lettuce blend

¾ cup (115 g) cherry tomatoes, halved

½ cup (120 ml) extra virgin olive oil

2 tbsp (6 g) fresh tarragon, minced

2 tbsp (30 ml) fresh lemon juice

1 shallot (2 tbsp [40 g]) minced

1 tbsp (15 ml) red wine vinegar

1 tbsp (15 g) Dijon mustard

Salt and pepper to taste

I love colorful summer salads, but even more so with ample amounts of bacon and croutons. You can find versions of Nüsslisalat throughout the Alps. It's great as a side or a main course.

When preparing bacon, I have the best technique for cooking it that prevents the messy splatter all over your stove top: I bake my bacon, and I bet it's a technique you will love too. I even used the bacon grease to toast the croutons. Bacon lovers look out—this will likely become your favorite salad!

*Serves 4–6*

To make the salad, preheat the oven to 400°F (205°C) with the rack in the middle. Cover a baking sheet with parchment paper or tin foil. Have a paper towel–lined plate and extra paper towels handy.

Place the bacon in a single layer on the baking sheet. Bake for 15 to 20 minutes or until the bacon is done to your liking. Cook time is also determined by the thickness of the bacon. Remove the bacon from the oven and, using a pair of tongs, place the bacon on the paper towel–lined plate. Soak up the extra grease with the paper towels. Keep the oven at 400°F (205°C). Do not get rid of the bacon grease, as you will use it for the croutons. Tear or cut the bacon into small pieces.

Place the bread on the sheet pan with the bacon grease. Gently rub both sides of the bread in the grease until well coated. Bake for about 15 minutes or until the bread is nice and toasted. Let cool a few minutes, then break with your hands or cut into cubes with a knife.

To make the dressing, place all of the ingredients into a lidded jar. Shake well until combined. Toss the salad with the dressing to serve.

# High Alpine Trout Salad with Creamy Shallot Dressing

## Trout

½ lb (230 g) fresh river trout, skin on, cut into 2 fillets

¼ cup (31 g) pistachios

Salt and pepper

2 tbsp (30 ml) olive oil

## Creamy shallot dressing

⅓ cup (80 ml) extra virgin olive oil

3 tbsp (45 ml) white wine vinegar

3 tbsp (45 g) mayonnaise

1 tbsp (15 g) Dijon mustard

1 shallot, rough chop

1 tsp honey

Salt and pepper to taste

## Salad

4 cups (120 g) baby spinach

¼ cup (40 g) golden raisins

⅓ cup (67 g) cherry or grape tomatoes, halved

Fishing is a favorite mountain activity. Whether you favor a spinner or a fly reel, there's one thing that's certain: there are plenty of wild mountain trout swimming around to tease your lure and tummy! This recipe can be served by the campfire or for a cozy meal at home.

*Serves 2*

To make the trout, give the pistachios a few quick pulses until you have a fine crumb in a food processor or blender. Don't over blend or you will end up with pistachio butter. Place the pistachios in a shallow bowl, add a pinch of salt and pepper and mix to combine. Place the trout fillets one at a time in the bowl and gently press the pistachios into the fillets on all sides.

Heat the oil in a cast-iron skillet over medium-high heat. Once it's hot (water drops will dance on the pan), place the trout skin side down. Cook for about 3 minutes, or until the bottom is golden brown. Flip the fish and cook another 2 to 5 minutes, depending on how well done you like your fish. If the pistachios start to burn, reduce the heat.

To make the dressing, combine all of the ingredients in a blender or food processor. Pulse until just combined.

Divide the spinach, raisins and tomatoes among the plates and place the trout on top. Drizzle with the dressing and serve.

# Wild Mushroom Ragout with Creamy Parmesan Polenta

## Wild mushroom ragout

¼ cup (60 ml) olive oil

1 yellow onion, finely chopped

2 cloves garlic, minced

1 lb (450 g) mixed wild mushrooms, cleaned and cut into bite-size pieces (varieties can include chanterelles, porcini, milkcaps, etc.)

½ cup (120 ml) dry white wine

2 tbsp (28 g) unsalted butter

2 tbsp (17 g) capers

2 cups (475 ml) low-sodium vegetable broth

1 tsp fresh rosemary, finely chopped

⅓ cup (80 ml) heavy cream

Salt and pepper to taste

¼ cup (6 g) fresh Italian parsley, finely chopped, plus more for serving

## Parmesan polenta

4 cups (950 ml) low-sodium vegetable stock

2 tsp (6 g) minced garlic (2 cloves)

1 cup (160 g) coarse yellow cornmeal

1 cup (100 g) freshly grated Parmesan cheese, plus extra for serving

¼ cup (60 ml) heavy cream

2 tbsp (28 g) unsalted butter

Salt and pepper to taste

There is a very special time in the mountains each year near the end of the summer. It's the annual mushroom harvest. This is when foragers hunt to find the most edible fungi. The haul can vary vastly as it all depends on mother nature's plans. Some years unleash thousands of pounds of chanterelles and assorted varieties. Other years, finding a handful is a big deal. Walking through town you hear the quiet buzz about where the wild mushroom stashes are. This, after all, is top-secret information for those on the hunt. Wild 'shrooms are so important to folks in Telluride that we even have a summer festival dedicated to them.

*Serves 4*

To make the ragout, heat the olive oil over medium heat in a 12-inch (30-cm) heavy-bottomed or cast-iron skillet until it's hot and shimmering. Add the onion and garlic. Cook for about 5 minutes, until soft and fragrant. Mix in the mushrooms. Sauté the mushrooms about 5 to 7 minutes so they soften and their juices evaporate, stirring often. Remove from the heat, add the white wine and stir to combine. Return to the heat and cook for 3 minutes to let the wine evaporate. Mix in the butter, capers, broth and rosemary, and simmer for 20 minutes or until the sauce is reduced by half. Stir in the cream. Heat another minute or so. Season with salt and pepper to taste. Remove from the heat to add fresh garnishes.

To make the polenta, place the veggie stock in a large saucepan. Add the garlic and cook over medium-high heat for 5 minutes, bringing the stock to a boil. Reduce the heat to medium-low, slowly pour in the cornmeal, whisking to make sure it doesn't get lumpy. Using a silicone spatula or wooden spoon, continue to stir the polenta. Scrape up any bits that start to collect on the bottom of the pan. Cook for about 10 minutes, stirring constantly. The polenta will be thick and creamy when done. Remove from the heat and mix in the Parmesan, cream and butter. Season with salt and pepper to taste.

Serve while hot. Place the mushroom ragout over the polenta. Sprinkle with fresh parsley and Parmesan cheese.

# Wurstsalat
## (Sausage and Cheese Salad)

The Germans know how to turn the idea of a traditional salad into a very creative culinary adventure. I've enjoyed this sausage and cheese salad throughout the Alps. Typically, it's mostly sliced meat, but I prefer it with lots of veggies for a full and hearty meal. It's just as delicious made with sliced hot dogs, bologna or sausage. It's simply dressed and gets most of its flavor from the chopped cured meat and alpine cheeses.

*Serves 8*

To make the dressing, whisk together all of the dressing ingredients.

To make the salad, combine all of the ingredients in a large bowl. Dress and season to taste.

### Dijon vinaigrette

¼ cup (60 ml) extra virgin olive oil

2 tbsp (30 ml) white wine vinegar

1 tbsp (15 ml) red wine vinegar

1 tbsp (15 g) Dijon mustard

1 tsp honey

Salt and pepper to taste

### Salad

1 head romaine lettuce or iceberg, chopped small

14 oz (400 g) German bologna (Fleischwurst), Swiss Cervelat sausage or boiled hot dogs, cut into bite-size pieces

1 red bell pepper, diced

½ red onion, minced

10 gherkins (mini pickles), sliced

7 oz (200 g) Gouda, Emmental or Gruyère cheese, cut into small cubes

# Savory Fare

There's always time to enjoy a delicious meal with family and friends. The summers are short and sweet, a special time for harvesting as much produce as you can for the cold and dark winter months. The warm growing season can be unpredictable—before you know it, snow can be falling from the sky. Fresh fruits and veggies are abundant in the summer, but not in the harsh alpine winters. Cheese and potatoes are common alpine fare all year-round; they are naturally able to fill you up and can be stored for a very long time. These hearty recipes make the most of rich and satisfying ingredients that give you plenty of energy for that next hike, bike or ski. They also nourish you perfectly for a chilly night tucked in under cozy down quilts.

# Chamonix Onion Soup Gratinée

## Soup

½ cup (114 g) unsalted butter

4 yellow onions, very thinly sliced

2 cloves garlic, smashed and chopped

¼ tsp sugar

2 tbsp (16 g) unbleached all-purpose flour

¼ cup (60 ml) dry white wine

3 tbsp (45 ml) cognac

8 cups (1.9 L) beef or vegetable stock

4 fresh thyme sprigs

1 bay leaf

Salt and freshly ground pepper, to taste

## Topping

1-lb (454-g) loaf of country-style white bread, cut into 1-inch (2.5-cm) thick slices

¾ cup (170 g) unsalted butter, melted

½ lb (230 g) grated Gruyère cheese

Chopped fresh parsley for garnish

Diving into a steamy bowl of French onion soup is the best thing ever! One of my favorite activities to do on a snowy winter's day is dine at chic mountain restaurants with my besties. Here in Telluride we have Bon Vivant, where we people watch, drink Champagne and enjoy hearty bowls of this soup. The melted Gruyère cheese topping is everything and is what makes this soup extra special. Whether on the slopes of Chamonix or in your dining room, this soup always brings on a cozy vibe.

*Serves 6*

To make the soup, melt the butter over medium-low heat in a large soup pot until any bubbling and foam has subsided. Add the onions, garlic and sugar. Cook over low heat for about 25 minutes until softened and caramelized, stirring often.

Stir in the flour. Cook for 2 minutes then add the wine and cognac, and cook for 5 minutes so they cook off a bit. Add the stock, thyme and bay leaf, bringing it to a boil. Partially cover the pot, then simmer and cook for 30 minutes. Skim occasionally if necessary. Add salt and pepper to taste. Remove the thyme and bay leaf, and discard.

To make the topping, preheat the oven to 350°F (180°C) while the soup is simmering. Place the bread on a baking sheet in a single layer. Brush both sides of the bread with the melted butter. Place in the oven and toast for 10 minutes, flipping halfway through.

Place six oven-proof soup bowls onto a baking tray. Transfer the soup to the bowls. Top each with a slice of bread, cheese and a drizzle of melted butter. Bake for 15 minutes; the soup should be simmering and the cheese melted. Broil for 2 to 3 minutes until the cheese has browned just a bit. Serve immediately, and garnish with parsley.

# Skillet Salmon with Creamy Lemon Thyme Sauce

## Salmon

Olive oil

½ lb (239 g) salmon fillets, divided into 2 portions, skin on

Salt and pepper

## Sauce

3 tbsp (45 ml) lemon juice

⅔ cup (160 ml) heavy cream

¼ cup (60 ml) dry white wine

2 cloves garlic, minced

2 tsp fresh thyme, minced

Salt and pepper to taste

## Garnish

Minced chives

Thyme sprigs

Lemon slices

From Sun Valley to British Columbia to Gstaad, salmon is a staple on mountain menus. This dish is just as perfect for a date night in as it is for a larger dinner party. It only takes minutes to throw it together, but the taste is elegant and very restaurant worthy! I've enjoyed variations of this salmon on alpine travels around the world. Whether the fish choice is trout, salmon or Arctic char it tastes wonderfully decadent and rustic all at the same time.

Serves 2

To make the salmon, rub olive oil on the fish and season both sides with salt and pepper.

To make the sauce, whisk together the lemon juice, cream, wine, garlic and thyme in a bowl.

Heat a splash of oil in an 8-inch (20-cm) cast-iron skillet over medium-high heat. Once the skillet is hot, place the fish on it, skin side down. Cook for 3 to 5 minutes until the skin is lightly browned and crispy. Flip the salmon and cook a few more minutes until the top is lightly browned. Cook according to preference, only 1 to 2 minutes for a more pink center. Remove the salmon from the pan and place on a plate. Turn off the heat. Let the pan cool for a few minutes.

Slowly pour the sauce into the skillet. It might splatter a bit so be careful. Turn the heat to low, and bring the sauce to a simmer. Stir the sauce while it's cooking; continue to cook about 10 minutes until the sauce has reduced by about half. Season to taste with salt and pepper.

Place the salmon back in the skillet for just a few minutes to reheat. Garnish with chives, thyme and lemon slices. Serve with a side of rice, potatoes or pasta and a fresh salad.

# Bunder Gerstensuppe
# (Swiss Barley Soup)

*2 tbsp (28 g) unsalted butter*

*2 tbsp (30 ml) olive oil*

*1 cup (150 g) onion, finely chopped*

*1 large leek, white part only, finely chopped*

*1 cup (150 g) carrots, peeled and finely diced (3 medium carrots)*

*1 cup (225 g) celery, finely diced (3 celery ribs)*

*5 oz (140 g) cooked bacon, finely chopped*

*8 cups (1.9 L) vegetable stock*

*1 cup (200 g) pearl barley*

*2 cups (450 g) russet potatoes, peeled and diced (2 medium potatoes)*

*Salt and pepper, to taste*

*1 cup (240 ml) heavy cream*

*¼ cup (6 g) chopped fresh parsley*

*Minced chives and more chopped parsley (for serving)*

One of my favorite U.S. backcountry ski guides recommended that I try this hearty, comfort food soup in a Swiss restaurant on the slopes of Davos. He said he waits all year to dive into a bowl of this creamy soup, exclaiming, "It's a religious experience!" No need to wait, friends, you can make a large pot of this family favorite at home any time you want it. This Swiss Barley Soup will warm you from the inside out. It's a full meal served with some crusty bread and maybe a wedge of cheese, too.

*Serves 4–6*

Heat the butter and oil in a Dutch oven or large soup pot over medium-high heat. Add the onion, leek, carrots and celery. Cook until softened and fragrant, about 10 minutes. Reduce the heat a bit if the onions start to brown too quickly. Add the bacon and cook for 2 minutes.

Add the stock, barley and potatoes. Simmer for 1 hour. Add salt and pepper to taste. If the soup seems too thick, add more water or stock. Stir in the cream, and bring the soup back to a simmer. Stir in the parsley. Serve while hot, topped with chives and fresh parsley.

# Badische Griessuppe
# (Semolina Soup)

2 tbsp (28 g) unsalted butter

3 tbsp (31 g) dry semolina or polenta

1 bunch green onions, small chop

3 carrots, peeled and cut into small cubes

2 cloves garlic, smashed and chopped

4 cups (950 ml) low-sodium vegetable broth

⅓ cup (80 ml) crème fraîche

1 large egg yolk

Salt, pepper and nutmeg to taste

¼ cup (6 g) chopped parsley plus some for garnish

Green onion for garnish

This rather light, vegetarian German soup will warm you from the inside out. It's a simple country farmhouse recipe in which you can use semolina or polenta and get the same results. Great for weeknight meals; serve with crusty bread, wedges of cheese and a fresh salad. I've enjoyed this soup in many ski chalets throughout Europe.

*Serves 4*

Melt the butter in a soup pot over medium heat. Add the semolina, cooking 1 minute until golden. Add the green onions, carrots and garlic, cooking about 3 minutes until fragrant and slightly softened. Add the broth, bringing it to a boil and simmering for 10 minutes; carrots should be soft. Reduce the heat to low.

Mix together the crème fraîche and the egg yolk. Add it to the soup, mixing constantly until well combined. Season to taste with salt, pepper and nutmeg. Stir in the ¼ cup (6 g) of parsley. Ladle the hot soup into bowls and top with some parsley and green onion.

# Raclette
# (Melted Cheese)

8 small or medium potatoes, or
16 fingerlings

Thinly sliced Bündnerfleisch, bresaola
or chipped beef

1 jar pickled cornichons

1 jar pickled onions

1½ lb (675 g) raclette cheese

Freshly ground pepper

Sweet paprika

My very first experience with raclette was in Switzerland overlooking the majestic Matterhorn. I had been skiing all day and was ravenous. This classic dish immediately became a favorite. In French, *racler* means "to scrape." Traditionally, a wheel of cheese is heated and then the melted part is scraped off. Whenever I smell raclette in a chalet I order it (yes, it has a very distinguishable smell!). Serve simply with cornichons, pickled onions, sliced Bündnerfleisch and boiled potatoes. I love to sip on white wine with it too—it washes it down nicely. There are special raclette machines and grills, but it's not necessary. I always use my handy cast-iron skillet!

*Serves 8*

Boil the potatoes for 20 minutes in well-salted water. Test if they are done with a knife. Drain the potatoes. On each plate, place a few potatoes, some Bündnerfleisch, a few cornichons and some pickled onions.

Remove the rind from the raclette cheese and with an adjustable wire cheese slicer, trim to ¼-inch (6-mm) slices.

Oil a 12-inch (30-cm) cast-iron skillet or a flat-top griddle. Heat over medium heat; when a splash of water sizzles, place a few cheese slices into the hot skillet. Melt the cheese and carefully scrape it onto the plates with a spatula. Sprinkle some pepper and paprika over the top and serve immediately.

# Garlic Roasted Beets and Potatoes

4 tbsp (57 g) unsalted butter

2 tbsp (30 ml) olive oil

2 tbsp (20 g) minced garlic (6 cloves)

2 tbsp (5 g) chopped thyme leaves

2 tbsp (5 g) chopped rosemary leaves

½ tsp kosher salt

½ tsp black pepper

1 lb (450 g) red beets, peeled and cubed

1 lb (450 g) red potatoes, cubed

It takes a thick skin to live in the mountains . . . that's why potatoes and beets do so well when stored in cold cellars. This recipe is a basic, but it's one I'm sure you will come back to over and over again. If you aren't already a beet lover, you will be after you try these!

*Serves 4*

Preheat the oven to 400°F (205°C) with the rack in the middle.

In a small saucepan melt the butter over medium-low heat. Add the oil, garlic, thyme, rosemary, salt and pepper. Sauté for 3 minutes.

Lay the beets and potatoes on a baking sheet side by side, keeping them all in a single layer. Drizzle the melted butter mixture over the top and toss with your hands, keeping beets and potatoes separate and in a single layer. Roast for 45 minutes or until the beets are softened. Toss with tongs halfway into the cooking time. Serve with your favorite protein and a fresh salad.

# La Tartiflette (Gratin)

2½ lb (1.2 kg) Charlotte potatoes (or any waxy salad potato), peeled

8 oz (230 g) bacon lardons or ½ lb (230 g) slab bacon cut into small dice

1 medium onion, thinly sliced

1 clove garlic, minced

¼ cup (60 ml) dry white wine

7 oz (240 ml) heavy cream

1 lb (450 g) Reblochon cheese, sliced

Fine salt and freshly ground black pepper

From the Savoy region in the French Alps, this delicious gratin is made with potatoes, cheese, cream and bacon—all readily available ingredients in high alpine farmhouses and ski resorts! Potatoes are belly filling and an easy starch to store in cellars for the long, dark winter months. Just like with the raclette (page 65), you can serve this dish with cornichons, pickled onions and Bündnerfleisch.

*Serves 4*

Preheat the oven to 400°F (205°C).

Boil the potatoes for 15 to 20 minutes or until easily pierced with a knife. Remove from the heat and set aside to cool. When cool enough to touch, cut into very thin slices.

In a 10-inch (25-cm) cast-iron skillet, cook the bacon lardons over medium-high heat until browned, about 10 minutes. Remove from the pan, leaving about 1 tablespoon (15 ml) of the bacon grease to cook the onion. Turn the heat to medium and cook the onion and garlic for 5 minutes, until soft and golden brown. Carefully add the bacon back in and the wine to the skillet. Cook another 5 minutes until most of the liquid has been absorbed.

Layer the potatoes and bacon mixture in an oven-proof 9 x 13-inch (23 x 33-cm) casserole dish or 9-inch (23-cm) round pie dish. Pour the cream over the top and place the cheese slices on top of that. Sprinkle with salt and pepper. Bake for 20 to 30 minutes or until the tartiflette is hot, the potatoes are soft and the cheese is golden brown and bubbling.

# Aelplermagronen
# (One-Pot Swiss Alpine Macaroni)

2 onions, sliced as thin as possible

2 cloves garlic, minced

10 oz (300 g) diced bacon

4½ cups (1.1 L) vegetable stock

1 cup (240 ml) half and half cream

1½ lb (680 g) waxy potatoes, diced into
½-inch (1.3-cm) pieces

1 lb (450 g) ziti pasta

6 oz (175 g) grated Gruyère cheese,
plus more for serving

Salt and pepper to taste

Fresh chopped parsley

Applesauce

One-pot meals are amazing, but they are even better when they are smothered in lots of melted cheese! Aelplermagronen is my all-time favorite mac 'n cheese recipe. I first tried it at the cozy Fuxägufer chalet in Davos, Switzerland, while soaking in the Graubuendner sunshine. This isn't just any mac, though; it's got slowly caramelized onions, plenty of bacon and lots of grated Gruyère cheese. This dish is full of big flavors. One thing that might sound kind of strange is it's served with a small bowl of applesauce on the side. This makes the dish extra amazing. Please don't go without it.

*Serves 4–6*

In a large soup pot or Dutch oven, cook the onions, garlic and bacon over medium heat for 25 to 30 minutes. You want the onions caramelized and the bacon cooked well. Stir often throughout the cooking time. Remove this mixture from the pan (including the oil from the bacon), place in a dish and set aside.

Add the stock, cream and potatoes to the pan. Increase the heat to medium-high, and bring to a boil. Add the pasta. Cover the pot with a lid and cook until the pasta is al dente, about 10 to 12 minutes. Once all the liquid is soaked into the pasta, remove the pan from the heat. Stir in the cheese, bacon and onion mixture. Season to taste with salt and pepper.

Serve with chopped parsley, applesauce and extra grated Gruyère.

# Elk Spaghetti Bolognese

1 tbsp (15 ml) olive oil (plus more for tossing pasta)

3 tbsp (43 g) unsalted butter

1 cup (150 g) chopped onion

⅔ cup (66 g) chopped celery

⅔ cup (100 g) chopped carrot

1 lb (450 g) ground elk, bison or beef

Salt and ground black pepper

1 cup (240 ml) whole milk

1 cup (240 ml) dry white wine

1½ cups (340 g) canned Italian plum tomatoes, pureed in a blender with the juices

1 lb (450 g) spaghetti, cooked to package directions, then tossed with olive oil

Freshly grated Parmigiano-Reggiano, Gruyère or Pecorino Romano cheese, for serving

When I'm in ski country, you can often find me sticking my face into a giant bowl of spaghetti Bolognese. I'll never forget a very sunny day on the outdoor patio of a restaurant in Lech, Austria—people watching, drinking a local white wine and inhaling spaghetti Bolognese. Always with extra cheese on the side! Game meats are very common in the high country. Ajax Tavern in Aspen has one of my all-time favorite Bolognese recipes on their menu. In the mountains, everyone knows someone who hunts and the bounty of delicious meat from a large elk or bison is the way to go for a full-flavored, protein-packed sauce.

*Serves 4*

Melt the oil and butter in a large saucepan or 12-inch (30-cm) cast-iron skillet over medium-high heat. Add the onion; cook until softened, translucent and fragrant, about 5 minutes. Add the chopped celery and carrot. Cook the veggies for about 3 minutes, making sure to stir well.

Add the ground elk with some salt and pepper. Stir the meat and break it up with a fork or spatula. Continue to cook and stir the meat until it is browned and cooked through, about 6 minutes. Add the milk, bringing the mix to a simmer. The milk should bubble until it virtually disappears, about 6 minutes. Add the wine, mix well and simmer until the wine evaporates, about 5 minutes. Add the tomatoes and bring to a low boil. Continue to cook over a very low temperature for about 1 hour, until the sauce thickens quite a bit. Stir every 10 to 15 minutes. Toss the sauce with spaghetti and serve with grated cheese.

This sauce tastes even better the next day as the flavors have a chance to really combine. A great make-ahead sauce!

# High Camp Champagne Cheese Fondue

1 clove garlic, peeled

1 tbsp (15 ml) fresh lemon juice

1 cup (240 ml) dry (brut) Champagne

8 oz (225 g) coarsely grated Gruyère cheese

8 oz (225 g) coarsely grated Emmental cheese

3 oz (85 g) Appenzeller cheese, cubed

4 tsp (13 g) cornstarch

1 tbsp (15 ml) kirsch

A few pinches of freshly ground nutmeg

Pinch of ground white pepper

### Serving

French baguette, crust left on, bread cut into 1-inch (2.5-cm) cubes

Cubed grilled steak

Lightly steamed vegetables

Apple slices

Cooked potatoes

Fondue is a staple skiers' food in the Alps and here in U.S. ski resorts. It's a stick-to-your-ribs dish meant to fill you up for the next run or next powder day. It's such a fun meal to share with friends for lunch, après or dinner. Dipping all kinds of goodies into melted cheese inspires all sorts of lively conversation! Serve with apple slices, steak, crusty French bread and fresh veggies. Don't forget the wine to drink, too.

*Serves 4*

Rub the inside of a cast-iron skillet with the garlic; discard the garlic when done.

Bring the lemon juice and Champagne to barely a simmer over medium heat. Combine the cheeses in a bowl with the cornstarch, making sure the cheeses are well coated.

A handful at a time, add the cheeses to the skillet, mixing until it's just melted. The mixture can bubble slightly, but do not boil. Continue to add the cheeses a handful at a time and stir until they are all melted. Stir in the kirsch, and season to taste with the nutmeg and pepper. Transfer the cheese to a fondue pot and keep it warm with the fondue burner. Serve with a baguette, steak, vegetables, apple slices and cooked potatoes for dipping.

# Giddy Up New York Strip with Garlic Smashed Red Bliss Potatoes

## Potatoes

2 lb (900 g) Red Bliss potatoes

4 tbsp (57 g) unsalted butter, melted

3 cloves garlic, smashed and minced

A few pinches of smoked paprika

Salt and ground black pepper to taste

## Steak

1 lb (450 g) New York strip steak

A few pinches garlic salt

A few pinches pepper

A few pinches smoked paprika

1 tbsp (14 g) unsalted butter

Freshly chopped Italian parsley

At the Glitretind at the Stein Eriksen Lodge in Park City, Utah, they have one of my all-time favorite steak dishes. I crave it every time I go there. This is my take on a classic cowgirl or cowboy meal. This dish is great for date night or anytime you have a craving for steak and potatoes!

*Serves 2–4*

To make the potatoes, preheat the oven to 450°F (230°C). Lightly oil a baking sheet with cooking spray. Bring a large pot of water to a boil, and add some salt and the potatoes. Cook for 15 to 20 minutes or until they are easy to pierce with a knife. Drain well.

Place the potatoes on the sheet pan. With a fork or potato masher, press on each potato until it is smashed, but still in one piece. Drizzle the butter and sprinkle the garlic over the potatoes. Bake for 18 to 20 minutes, until golden brown and crispy. Remove from the oven and season to taste with some smoked paprika, salt and pepper.

To make the steak, season both sides of the steak with garlic salt, pepper and smoked paprika while the potatoes are baking. Heat the butter in a grill pan or cast-iron skillet over medium-high heat. When it's sizzling, place the steak in the pan and cook 4 to 6 minutes until the bottom has a nicely browned crust. Flip the steak and continue to cook until the desired level of doneness is attained. Serve immediately with the potatoes. Garnish with parsley.

# Roasted Tomato Soup with Grilled Cheese Croutons

## Soup

Olive oil

1 onion, diced small

2 cloves garlic, minced

2 (15-oz [425-g]) containers vegetable stock

1 (28-oz [795-g]) can fire-roasted crushed tomatoes

½ cup (120 ml) milk

½ cup (120 ml) heavy cream

1 tsp smoked paprika

Salt and black pepper to taste

Chopped basil, parsley or cilantro for garnish

## Grilled cheese croutons

Unsalted butter for frying

4 slices whole-wheat bread

Mayonnaise

4 slices cheddar cheese (you can also use Gruyère, Emmental or Appenzeller cheese for an Alps twist)

Tomato soup and grilled cheese are the best, but put them together and you have the ultimate alpine feast! Serve this up any night of the week and I'm certain your entire family will love you even more than ever. I can't think of any mountain town that doesn't have a delicious tomato soup on the menu. This, though, is the best combo I've ever had!

*Serves 8*

To make the soup, add a good splash of olive oil to a soup pot and heat the onion and garlic over medium heat. Cook for a few minutes until fragrant and softened, about 5 minutes. Add the stock and tomatoes. Bring to a boil then reduce the heat to medium-low, stirring in the milk and heavy cream. Season with the smoked paprika and some salt and pepper to taste. Simmer gently for 15 minutes, stirring occasionally. Puree the soup with an immersion blender or regular blender.

To make the grilled cheese croutons, heat a generous pat of butter in a frying pan over medium heat. Make sandwiches with the bread, slather on some mayonnaise and layer on the cheese. Fry the sandwiches for a few minutes on each side until golden brown and crispy, 2 minutes per side. Slice sandwiches into cubes/croutons.

Serve hot bowls of soup with grilled cheese croutons floating on the top.

# Pork Überschnitzel

6 boneless top pork loin chops (½ inch [1.3 cm] thick, 1½ lb [675 g]), trim off excess fat

⅓ cup (42 g) unbleached all-purpose flour

1 tsp dried oregano

½ tsp salt

½ tsp ground black pepper

½ tsp garlic powder

1 cup (90 g) panko bread crumbs

1 large egg

¼ cup (60 ml) milk

3 tbsp (45 ml) vegetable oil

The first time I indulged in Wiener Schnitzel was at a private chef's tasting at the five-star Badrutt's Palace in St. Moritz, Switzerland. It was an unforgettable experience, as I spent the day with the executive chefs in the vast hotel kitchen. I photographed them all day then was asked to sit down and enjoy their culinary creations. It was very exciting, and I've never seen so much food on one table! The Wiener Schnitzel was a total win. You can make it with pork or veal, but I prefer the pork.

*Serves 6*

Spread plastic wrap or waxed paper on a clean work surface and loosely wrap the pork in it. Pound with a meat mallet until the chops are the thinnest you can get them, ⅛- to ¼-inch (3- to 6-mm) thick cutlets. Season both sides with some salt and pepper.

In a large, shallow bowl, whisk the flour with the oregano, salt, pepper and garlic powder. Place the bread crumbs in another large, shallow bowl. In another bowl, beat the egg with the milk. Working one at a time, dip each pork chop first into the flour, shake off the excess, then into the egg, letting the excess drip off before dipping it into the panko. Press the panko crumbs in to coat.

Heat the oil in a 12-inch (30-cm) cast-iron skillet over medium-high heat until it shimmers. Place a few cutlets in the skillet and cook a few minutes until each is golden brown and crispy, about 3 minutes. Flip and cook the other side. Continue to cook the rest of the cutlets, adding more oil as needed to the pan; you want the crust to be golden brown. Serve immediately.

# Colorado Lamb with Cinnamon Chimayó Chile Rub

Spice rub

2 tbsp (16 g) mild Chimayó chile powder

1 tbsp (16 g) pure cane sugar

1 tsp ground cinnamon

½ tsp garlic powder

½ tsp black pepper

½ tsp salt

Lamb

4 lamb chops

Grapeseed oil

Colorado cuisine celebrates lamb in so many different ways. My favorite is simply grilled or sautéed in a super-hot cast-iron skillet. This spice rub makes all the difference, adding flavor but keeping the hearty flavor of the lamb intact. Chimayó is a chile pepper found in New Mexico near the high mountains of Santa Fe. The male is the milder version, whereas the female pepper is hot and spicy. Choose how much heat you crave. This lamb is just as fabulous served at a dinner party as it is in front of the campfire.

*Serves 2–4*

To make the spice rub, combine the chile powder, sugar, cinnamon, garlic powder, pepper and salt and muddle together with the back of a spoon or mortar and pestle.

To make the lamb, pat the lamb chops dry with paper towels. Liberally rub the spice mix into each chop, making sure all sides are covered well.

Heat a few tablespoons of the oil in a grill pan or 12-inch (30-cm) cast-iron skillet over medium-high heat. Gently place the chops in the pan, taking care as the oil might splatter. Cook 4 minutes on the first side and 4 to 5 minutes on the second side. Add more seasoning as you see fit. Remove from the skillet and serve immediately.

Note: *Lamb chops come in different thicknesses. Make sure your lamb is cooked to your liking before serving. If you use an instant-read thermometer, 155°F (68°C) is medium doneness.*

# Krautfleckerl
# (Pasta with Caramelized Cabbage)

2 cups (200 g) dry egg pasta, or more as desired

4 tbsp (57 g) unsalted butter

1 yellow onion, chopped

1 tbsp (14 g) sugar

1 tsp salt

½ tsp ground black pepper

4 cups (400 g) chopped cabbage

Chopped fresh parsley for topping

I first experienced this delicious sautéed pasta dish at a chic mountain restaurant called the Hospitz Alm, located slope side in the charming village of St. Cristoph, Austria. I'll never forget the picture-perfect bluebird Arlberg day. This is a vast area of the Austrian Alps of which there are five distinct charming alpine villages that are all connected by a user-friendly gondola and chairlift system. It's known to be the birthplace of the alpine ski technique as we know it today. The ski moves are just as beautiful as are the flavors of the food. These noodles are sure to satisfy hungry tummies no matter what your activity! I knew when I got back to the United States it would become an immediate family favorite.

*Serves 4*

Cook the pasta according to package directions and set aside. Melt the butter in a large, heavy-bottomed Dutch oven or cast-iron skillet over medium-high heat. Add the onion. Reduce the heat to medium and cook the onion for 10 minutes, until softened and fragrant, stirring occasionally.

Add the sugar, salt, pepper and cabbage, cooking for 10 minutes. Stir occasionally, until the cabbage is soft and golden. It's good to have some slightly brown parts. Add the pasta into the pan and combine well. Top with some fresh parsley.

# Pizokel from Graubünden

1 cup (120 g) buckwheat flour

1 cup (125 g) unbleached
all-purpose flour

Pinch of salt and ground black pepper

2 large eggs

½ cup (120 ml) milk

½ cup (120 ml) water

½ cup (75 g) chopped Bündnerfleisch
or ham, cut into small pieces

Various seasonal vegetables, chopped
into bite-size pieces

Unsalted butter

Grated alpine cheese such as Gruyère,
Appenzeller or raclette

Pizokel is an alpine staple in the Graubünden (Grisons) canton of Switzerland. This area is entirely mountainous with over 2,700 square miles of alpine wonders! Ski resorts include Arosa, Lenzerheide, Davos Klosters, St. Moritz and more. The views are absolutely breathtaking no matter where you go. Climb or take a chairlift to any peak and you will be mesmerized by the natural beauty. Take in the Piz-Bernina, the highest peak in the region, while you enjoy a steaming plate of Pizokel. These buckwheat flour dumplings are a wholesome and truly satisfying meal. Add in as many seasonal veggies that you have on hand.

*Serves 4*

In a large bowl, whisk together the flours, salt and pepper. In a smaller bowl, whisk the eggs with milk and water. Add the egg mixture into the flour. Mix to combine with a silicone spatula. Fold in the Bündnerfleisch. Let the dough sit for 30 minutes.

Bring a large soup pot of water to a boil (filled about half way.) Rinse a wooden cutting board with cold water. With a spatula, spread the dough onto the board to be ¼ inch (6 mm) thick, making sure the dough hits the edge of the board.

Add the veggies to the pot. Lean the cutting board against the side of the pot. With a knife, start slicing small amounts of dough into the boiling water. At this point you can determine what size you want your dumplings to be. Continue to add the dough until it's all used up. Boil everything for about 4 minutes, or until the dumplings are all floating on the top.

Drain the veggies and dumplings, and toss with the butter and cheese. Serve immediately topped with more butter, Bündnerfleisch and cheese.

# Spinach Knödels
# (Spinatknödel)

10 slices day-old store-bought bread, crusts removed

¾ cup (180 ml) milk

1 tbsp (14 g) unsalted butter

½ yellow onion, chopped small

1 tsp salt

½ tsp ground black pepper

3 cups (90 g) loosely packed baby spinach

1 clove garlic, minced

2 large eggs, whisked

⅓ cup (42 g) all-purpose flour

Melted butter

Parmesan cheese

I first experienced these dumplings (knödels) when I was trekking the Italian Dolomites. This is a regional dish that is popular in the South Tyrol, which is a majestic part of the Alps that borders between Northern Italy and Austria. The food is a combination of the two distinct alpine cultures.

Put on your lederhosen and eat some knödels! There are many varieties; I chose the spinach ones because I love the extra serving of veggies in these. The traditional topping is Parmesan cheese and lots of butter. Feel free to experiment with your veggie fillings. These dumplings are equally delicious served with butter or in a light vegetable broth as a soup.

*Serves 4–6*

Your bread should be somewhat stale for this recipe. To get those results quickly, preheat the oven to 400°F (205°C). Lay bread slices on a sheet pan in a single layer. Toast for 5 to 8 minutes, or until bread is just firm. Break the bread into pieces and soak in the milk while the onion cooks.

Melt the butter in a heavy-bottomed skillet. Cook the onion over low heat about 10 minutes, until fragrant, golden and softened. Stir often, seasoning with the salt and pepper. Steam the spinach, then chop it into small pieces. Add the spinach to the onion. Combine well. Remove the skillet from the heat. Add the onion, spinach and garlic to the milk-drenched bread. Mix in the eggs and flour.

Take 2 tablespoons (27 g) of the mix and with damp hands roll it into balls. Boil a large pot of water and cook knödels for 15 minutes. Remove from the pot with a slotted spoon.

Serve with melted butter and Parmesan cheese.

*See photo on page 54.

# Spaetzle with Pheasant and Swiss Chard Pesto

### Pheasant

¼ cup (60 ml) grapeseed oil

1 tbsp (14 g) unsalted butter

2 pheasants (1¾–2 lb [750–900 g] each), cleaned and oven-ready, preferably hens

Fine sea salt and ground black pepper

### Spaetzle

2 cups (250 g) all-purpose flour

2 tsp (10 g) salt

1 tsp black pepper

2 tsp dried thyme

4 large eggs

½ cup (120 ml) milk, plus extra if needed

### Swiss chard pesto

2 packed cups (75 g) roughly chopped Swiss chard, leaves only

½ cup (50 g) shaved aged Pecorino Romano cheese

1 clove garlic, roughly chopped

½ cup (120 ml) olive oil

½ tsp salt (more to taste)

2 tbsp (30 ml) freshly squeezed lemon juice

¼–½ cup (50–75 g) toasted pecans

### Sauté

3 tbsp (43 g) unsalted butter

3 tbsp (45 ml) olive oil

2 shallots, minced

Spaetzle are traditional German egg noodle dumplings that you find at many alpine restaurants. This is a well-rounded meal that your entire family will love. Spaetzle has a nice chewy texture, and it is wonderful paired with pheasant and this Swiss chard pesto. On fall weekends I love to venture out to Delta, Colorado, and hunt for pheasant. Working with the dogs is always a treat, and hunting for our own food is a wonderful feeling. If you don't hunt, many markets carry pheasant either at the butcher or in the frozen case. It's a very lean bird and does not need to be cooked too long. If you cannot find it, you can easily swap in darker cuts of chicken.

*Serves 2*

To make the pheasant, preheat the oven to 375°F (190°C).

Heat the oil and butter in a 12-inch (30-cm) cast-iron skillet over medium heat. Once the butter is bubbling, lay the pheasants in the pan legs side down; cook until golden brown, 2 to 3 minutes, and then flip to the breast side. Cook another 2 to 3 minutes until golden brown. Season with salt and pepper. Transfer the pan to the oven and bake for 30 minutes, turning halfway through cook time. When cooked, shred the pheasant and set aside to rest in a warm place until ready to use.

To make the spaetzle, combine the flour, salt, pepper and thyme in a large bowl. In another smaller bowl combine the eggs and milk. Make a well in the center of the flour mixture, and pour in the egg mixture. Using a fork, combine to form a dough, working the flour in from the edges. Once the dough is well combined, it should be smooth and thick. The consistency needs to be doughy, but thin enough to press through a colander (the holes should be on the larger side) or potato ricer. Add milk as needed. Let sit at room temperature for 10 to 15 minutes.

To make the pesto, place all of the pesto ingredients in a blender or food processor and blend until well combined. Taste and adjust any seasonings to taste.

(continued)

Bring a large pot of salted water to a boil, then simmer. Place a colander over the pot, pour the spaetzle dough into the chosen device. If using a colander, press the dough through the holes with the back of a wooden spoon. The shapes do not need to be consistent. Keep pressing until you have pressed all the dough through. Simmer for 3 to 4 minutes. Drain in a clean colander. Rinse with cold water so they stop cooking.

To make the sauté, heat the butter and olive oil in a 12-inch (30-cm) cast-iron skillet over medium-low heat. When it's sizzling, add the shallots. Cook for 5 minutes until fragrant and softened. Add the spaetzle to the pan. Cook for 3 minutes until hot, stirring often so the mixture doesn't stick. Remove from the heat when done.

Using the same skillet that the spaetzle is in, turn the heat to medium-low. Add some pesto and the shredded pheasant. Gently mix to combine, adding as much pesto and pheasant as you like, heat until hot, about 5 minutes. Serve immediately.

Note: *You can use a meat thermometer to make sure the pheasants are properly cooked. The breast temperature for a cock pheasant should reach 145°F (63°C) and 140°F (60°C) for a hen. The leg temperature should reach 175° to 180°F (80° to 82°C).*

# Après All Day

Rosé all day and après all day. These are two common sayings you hear on and off the pistes. In the mountains, no party is too small and no time of day is off limits for fun. These bites are suitable for all kinds of gatherings.

Traditionally we know the late afternoon in the winter to be time for après ski. But in the warmer months, it's the same calling. These recipes are appetizers that are meant to satisfy hungry bellies. How fun is it to meet up with friends after a bomber day on the slopes to exchange stories from the day? No après is complete without luscious libations (page 151).

# Powder Day Flatbread with Prosciutto and Arugula

Extra virgin olive oil

2 pita flatbreads

6 oz (170 g) sliced fresh mozzarella cheese

2 cloves garlic, smashed and minced

¼ cup (25 g) thinly sliced red onion

¼ cup (14 g) julienned sun-dried tomatoes in oil

6 slices prosciutto

2 handfuls arugula

¼ cup (25 g) shaved Parmesan

Freshly ground pepper

Flatbreads and all kinds of pizzas are always a great match for a fireside feast. They smell so good as they bake and always beckon ravenous powder hounds in to eat. These take only minutes to throw together and are perfect for weeknight meals and entertaining. Elevate your next flatbread experience with these belly-filling bites.

*Serves 2*

Preheat the oven to 400°F (205°C) with the rack in the middle. Rub some olive oil on a baking sheet. Place the flatbreads on the sheet. Rub some olive oil onto the tops of the flatbreads. Divide the mozzarella, garlic, onion, sun-dried tomatoes and prosciutto evenly on top of the flatbreads.

Bake for 10 minutes then broil, watching carefully for 2 to 3 minutes. The cheese should be bubbling and the crust edges brown and crispy. Remove the flatbreads from the oven, transfer to plates, and top with the arugula, shaved Parmesan and pepper. Serve immediately.

# Alps Cheese and Charcuterie Board

## Alpine cheeses

*These are just a few suggestions; talk to your local fromagiere to see what they have on hand. You can also find many items at online markets. Try for a mixture of soft and firm goat, cow and sheep cheeses.*

Abondance

Appenzeller

Beaufort

Bra Duro

Comte

Emmental

Fontina Val D'Aosta

Gruyère

Prättigauer

Raclette

## Alpine charcuterie

*For the meat selections, try to get some variety in flavor, texture and animal choice. Talk to your local butcher and also find unique items online. Here are a few suggestions:*

Bündnerfleisch

Landjäger

Paté

Prosciutto

Salami

Saucisson

Speck

One of my all-time favorite things is a decadent cheese and charcuterie board. Charcuterie meats are derived from the preservation process that has been perfected over hundreds of years. I've enjoyed my most favorite displays in the Alps, but the U.S. alpine areas are quickly catching up.

Nothing beats making a cheese and charcuterie board at home. You can be as creative as you want; I always say, wow guests with the best! I prefer alpage cheeses as the cows are feeding off the most pristine pastures, and the flavors are full and rich. There is such care and tradition in the making of these cheeses.

A few rules of thumb you want when creating an epic cheese and meat platter:

**Serving size:** Figure on 1 to 2 oz (28 to 56 g) of meat and the same for cheese per person if serving as an appetizer; serve more of each for a main dish.

**Textures:** Add interest with a variety of textures, including creamy, crunchy, chewy, soft and firm.

**Flavors:** Run the gamut with sweet, salty, spicy and savory.

**Serving elements:** Each cheese should have its own knife so flavors don't combine. Have plenty of crackers, veggie and edible serving vehicles at the ready.

**Know what you are serving:** Have cheese markers available or be prepared to explain the board.

Cheese and charcuterie boards should be served at room temperature.

You only need three to five cheese and meat variations per board. Don't over-do it—that just gets confusing.

One of the most exciting elements to any spectacular cheese and charcuterie board is the element of surprise. It's where sweet and salty and different textures come alive. Add nuts, dried fruits, fresh fruits and dips. Try the Fig Jam on page 98.

The biggest rule is don't be shy and go for the win! What I love most about these boards is the conversation that happens around them. Make sure to serve plenty of red and white wine and bubbles for the most lively conversation.

# Fig Jam

8 oz (225 g) fresh figs, cleaned and chopped small

½ cup (100 g) sugar

2 tbsp (28 ml) fresh lemon juice, divided

1 tsp pure vanilla extract

This is one of my favorite condiments for an Alps board. I love how the sweetness pairs with the salty, briny and savory flavors of the cheeses and meats.

*Makes 1 cup (230 g)*

In a medium saucepan, bring the figs, sugar, 1 tablespoon (15 ml) of the lemon juice and vanilla to a simmer over medium-low heat, stirring often. Cover the pot and simmer over low heat for about 12 to 15 minutes, stirring very often; you want to make sure the jam doesn't stick to the bottom of the pan. The jam will be quite thick when done. Transfer the jam to a blender or food processor, add the remaining 1 tablespoon (15 ml) of lemon juice and mix until well combined. Store in an airtight jar in the refrigerator until ready to serve.

# Après Ski Three-Cheese Spinach Artichoke Dip

1 (8-oz [225-g]) block cream cheese, room temperature

1 cup (100 g) freshly grated Parmesan cheese

1 cup (115 g) shredded cheddar cheese

2 oz (60 g) diced pimento, drained well

2 oz (60 g) diced green chiles, drained well

¼ tsp garlic powder

1 (14-oz [425-g]) jar marinated artichoke hearts, chopped

1 (10-oz [280-g]) package frozen spinach, thawed and squeeze out any liquid

In the mountains we are obsessed with cheese—hot melty cheese to be exact. In the Alps it's fondue and raclette. Stateside, artichoke dip takes center stage. Artichokes and cheese go together like puffy jackets and knit hats. They are a simple, mouthwatering combo that has taken over appetizer menus everywhere. What is it about a hot, gooey cheese dip that melts hearts? It must be the decadence and rich flavors. For color and a little more pizzazz in my dip, I add diced pimentos and for a little heat, some diced green chiles.

*Serves 4–6*

Preheat the oven to 350°F (180°C).

In a bowl, combine the cheeses, pimento, chiles and garlic powder using a wooden spoon. Fold in the artichokes and spinach. Transfer to an oven-safe pie plate or dish. Bake 30 to 40 minutes until the dip is golden brown. Serve with pita chips, sliced French bread, crackers or sliced fresh veggies.

*See photo on page 92.

# Black Diamond Bratwurst with Sauerkraut and Onions

2 tbsp (30 ml) vegetable oil

5 beer bratwurst

1½ yellow onions, sliced into thick rings

2 cloves garlic, minced

3 cups (700 ml) low-sodium chicken broth

1 tbsp (15 ml) maple syrup

1½ lb (680 g) sauerkraut

1 tbsp (7 g) paprika

1 tbsp (9 g) dried dill

2 tbsp (5 g) freshly chopped parsley for garnish

This is a wonderfully filling meal that is reminiscent of many I have enjoyed in the Alps, Canadian Rockies and the United States. It's a hearty dish that is made even better served around the fire with a fur blanket. Don't forget the chilled lager to balance everything out. A big day on the slopes makes you super thirsty and ravenous!

*Serves 5*

In a 12-inch (30-cm) cast-iron skillet, heat the oil over medium-high heat, cook the bratwurst until browned on all sides. Reduce the heat to medium, adding the onion and garlic. Cook until lightly browned and caramelized, about 12 minutes; toss the mixture with a pair of tongs to make sure it cooks evenly. Add the broth, maple syrup, sauerkraut, paprika and dill. Bring to a boil, then simmer for 45 minutes. Serve immediately, garnished with freshly chopped parsley.

# Buffalo Chicken Meatballs

4 tbsp (57 g) unsalted butter

⅓ cup (80 ml) hot sauce (such as Frank's RedHot)

⅓ cup (83 g) crumbled blue cheese, plus more for serving

Pinch of kosher salt and black pepper

⅓ cup (30 g) panko bread crumbs

1 celery rib, chopped (½ cup [50 g])

½ cup (45 g) finely chopped carrot

2 cloves garlic, minced

1 shallot, minced

1 large egg

1 lb (450 g) ground chicken

Extra virgin olive oil

Sliced green onion

Italian parsley

This twist on buffalo chicken wings is both playful and delicious (not to mention you don't have to get your hands dirty eating them!). It's a tasty, fun appetizer to share with friends for après-ski, happy hour or game day. I've had versions of tasty meatballs on many high peaks; these are my all-time favorite inspired by the Black Iron Kitchen and Bar in Telluride, Colorado.

*Serves 8*

Preheat the oven to 425°F (220°C). Heat the butter, hot sauce, blue cheese, salt and pepper in a small saucepan over medium heat. Whisk to combine well, cooking about 2 minutes. Remove from the heat and let cool.

Mix together the bread crumbs, celery, carrot, garlic, shallot and egg in a bowl. Add the chicken and half of the hot sauce mixture. Mix until just combined, but do not over mix.

Coat a 10-inch (25-cm) cast-iron skillet with olive oil, using a paper towel or brush. Form 1-inch (2.5-cm) meatballs and place in the prepared skillet in a single layer. Drizzle with some more olive oil. Bake until the meatballs are lightly golden brown, 15 to 17 minutes.

Warm the rest of the sauce and drizzle over the meatballs. Top with green onions, parsley and some blue cheese. Serve with toothpicks or small cocktail forks.

# Chalet Truffle Fries with Grated Alpine Cheese

3 large russet potatoes, peeled

Peanut oil for frying

1–2 tbsp (15–30 ml) truffle oil

Fine salt to taste

One or a combination of grated Gruyère, raclette, Appenzeller and Emmental cheeses

Chopped fresh herbs (rosemary, thyme, oregano)

Truffle fries . . . you smell them as soon as you walk into an alpine restaurant. In the Alps you will likely smell cheesy raclette or fondue first, but in the United States it's truffle fries and burgers. You can find this finger food on most menus throughout the high country. Why? Because truffle fries are pretty much the best way to take in calories after you've burnt so many on the ski hill. I always order these at The 10th and Sweet Basil in Vail and Ajax Tavern in Aspen . . . or actually everywhere they are offered on the menu!

*Serves 6*

Prepare two baking sheets by lining them with paper towels.

Cut the potatoes into ⅜-inch (8-mm) thick fries. I like to use a knife best for this to create perfectly straight, perfectly crispy and completely delicious fries. Soak the cut potatoes in a large, non-reactive bowl of cold water for 30 minutes. Remove and pat dry with paper towels.

In a heavy-bottomed pot, heat 3 to 4 inches (7.5 to 10 cm) of the peanut oil. Using a candy thermometer, make sure the temperature is 325°F (165°C). Do not let the thermometer rest on the bottom of the pan as you will get a misread.

Add the potatoes in small batches, so the oil temperature is not affected. Cook for 5 to 6 minutes. Turn with a pair of tongs; they will not brown much at this stage. Transfer the fries to the paper towel–lined trays. Let cool a few minutes.

Raise the temperature of the oil to 375°F (190°C). Fry until crisp and golden to your liking, only 1 to 2 minutes longer. Remove the fries from the oil and let drain again on the paper towels. Drizzle on the truffle oil, and season with a touch of salt to taste. Toss with the tongs and transfer to a serving dish. Top with preferred cheeses and herbs.

Note: *Truffle oil comes in many varieties. Some are more pure than others. Add it slowly to your fries and taste as you go.*

# Croque Madame with Béchamel Sauce

## Béchamel sauce

1 tbsp (14 g) unsalted butter

1 tbsp (8 g) unbleached all-purpose flour

⅔ cup (160 ml) whole milk

Pinch of salt

Pinch of nutmeg

½ cup (50 g) grated Gruyère cheese

## Sandwiches

4 slices white bread, crusts removed

8 thin slices ham

2 tbsp (28 g) unsalted butter, plus some more for the eggs

⅓ cup (33 g) grated Gruyère cheese

2 large eggs

Hungry bellies crave cheese and that's all there is to it. Add some ham, lots of butter and béchamel sauce and you have heaven on a plate. You can find versions of this chic baked sandwich at cafes and chalets all over the globe. I always stop mid-mountain in Telluride at everyone's favorite outdoor restaurant, Bon Vivant, for a croque and a flute of Champagne.

*Serves 2*

To make the béchamel sauce, melt the butter in a saucepan over medium heat. Whisk in the flour and cook for 2 to 3 minutes, stirring constantly until you smell the flour/butter cooking. Do not let it brown. Whisk in the milk, salt and nutmeg, and cook for about 10 minutes or until the sauce thickens. With a spatula, mix in the cheese. Taste and adjust any seasonings if needed. Remove the sauce from the heat and transfer to a bowl.

To make the sandwiches, preheat the broiler. Lay the bread on a work surface. Spread béchamel sauce on one side of each slice. Top two of these pieces of bread with four slices of ham each. Top with the two remaining slices of bread.

Heat the 2 tablespoons (28 g) of butter in a 10-inch (25-cm) cast-iron skillet over medium heat. When it starts sizzling, add the sandwiches to the pan. Cook for a few minutes on each side, so the cheese melts and the bread turns golden brown. Spread some more béchamel on the tops of the sandwiches. Top each with the Gruyère cheese. Take the cast-iron skillet and move it into the oven. Broil 2 to 3 minutes until the cheese is browned.

While the sandwiches are cooking, make the eggs. Heat a pat of butter in another skillet over medium heat. When it's sizzling, add the eggs. Cook for 3 to 4 minutes until the whites turn opaque. Remove from the heat and place on the top of the croques. Cook longer if you like your eggs firmer.

# Massif Bretzels with Crusty Gruyère Topping

1½ cups (350 ml) warm water (lukewarm; you do not need to take the temperature)

1 tbsp (14 g) sugar

1 (¼-oz [7-g]) package active dry yeast

2 tbsp (28 g) unsalted butter, melted and slightly cool

4–4½ cups (500–563 g) all-purpose flour, plus more for work surface

1 large egg, whisked with 1 tbsp (15 ml) water

8 oz (230 g) grated Gruyère cheese

10 cups (2.4 L) cold water

⅔ cup (146 g) baking soda

Coarse pretzel salt

As soon as I take off or land at the Zurich, Switzerland airport, the first thing I run for is my favorite Brezelkönig (Pretzel King) soft pretzels. These are not your average soft pretzels. They are massive, and there is every topping you could possibly imagine on offer. You can order a simple buttered bretzel or go for the pumpkin seed crusted ones. You can even order a Bretzel Bündnerfleisch sandwich. I love the cheese-smothered bretzels, Gruyère and raclette always being favorites.

This alpine classic is a hearty snack, made even more perfect served with a chilled stein of beer.

*Makes 12 pretzels*

In the bowl of a stand mixer, whisk together the warm water, sugar, yeast and butter. Let sit for 5 minutes or until foaming. Using the dough hook, add the flour into the bowl in two additions. Mix on low then turn the speed to medium. The dough should begin to pull away from the sides, poke the dough and it should bounce back. If it's very sticky, add a bit more flour. Transfer the dough to a floured surface. Knead the dough and shape into a ball. Place the dough in a well-oiled (vegetable oil) large bowl covered with plastic wrap and let sit in a warm place for about 50 to 55 minutes. It will double in size.

Preheat the oven to 400°F (205°C). Line two baking sheets with parchment paper. Lightly brush or spray with some vegetable oil. Get the egg wash and cheese ready.

Bring the cold water and baking soda to a rolling boil in a large soup pot. Place the dough onto a floured work surface. Divide it into 12 pieces. Roll each piece out with your hands to make a 22-inch (56-cm) rope. Make a "U" shape with the rope. Cross the tips over one another, then bring them toward you, gently pressing them into the base of the pretzel.

With a slotted spatula, gently place each pretzel, one at a time, into the boiling water for 20 to 30 seconds. Place onto the baking sheet. Brush with egg wash, and sprinkle on some salt and cheese. Bake for 12 to 15 minutes, until the cheese and pretzels are golden brown. Transfer to a cooling rack for 5 minutes before serving.

# Rancher's Bison Sliders with Bacon Aioli and Caramelized Onions

## Caramelized onions

2 tbsp (28 g) unsalted butter

2 tbsp (27 g) vegetable oil

2 yellow onions, cut to your desired level of thickness

Salt and pepper to taste

## Bacon aioli

5 strips baked bacon, finely chopped

½ cup (120 g) mayonnaise

2 cloves garlic, chopped

2 tbsp (30 ml) fresh lemon juice

Salt and pepper to taste

## Burgers

1 lb (454 g) ground bison (or lean chopped meat)

2 cloves garlic, minced

1 tbsp (3 g) freshly chopped parsley

¼ tsp salt

¼ tsp black pepper

6 slider buns or dinner rolls

In the western U.S. ski country, bison can be a locally sourced meat and is always a favorite. From Jackson Hole to Aspen to Telluride, this is a ranch fixture from state to state. Bison sliders are as great as a powder day (well, almost!). Topped with rustic, smoky bacon aioli and caramelized onions, these will be popular so make sure you cook up a few per person as they don't last long. Be sure to honor the time it takes to caramelize onions—it's well worth it. I promise!

*Makes 6 sliders*

To make the caramelized onions, melt the butter and heat the oil in a 12-inch (30-cm) cast-iron skillet over medium heat. Add the onions, salt and pepper, making sure the onions cover the entirety of the pan. Stir well. Cook for 45 minutes, stirring very often. If you see the onions cooking too quickly, reduce the temperature. Transfer the onions to a bowl. You will use this pan for the bison too; do not rinse it.

To make the aioli, mix together the bacon, mayonnaise, garlic and lemon juice in a bowl. Season with salt and pepper to taste.

To make the burgers, combine the bison with the garlic, parsley, salt and pepper. Form six patties and place the burgers in the skillet over medium-high heat. Cook for 3 to 4 minutes per side, depending on how well done you prefer your sliders.

To assemble, spread the aioli onto both sides of the bun. Place the burger on the bottom half, topping with the caramelized onions and top of the bun. Serve immediately.

# Brown Butter Chicken Wings with Smoked Paprika and Fresh Herbs

6 tbsp (85 g) unsalted butter

4 cloves garlic, minced

2 tsp (5 g) smoked paprika

2 lb (900 g) chicken wings

Kosher salt and black pepper

Chopped fresh herbs: thyme, oregano or your favorite combination

Whether you are saddled up to the bar for game day or coming off the snowy slopes, one thing is for certain: it's these wings for the win. There's nothing like sitting down to a stack of sizzling chicken wings. Have a stack of napkins at the ready, as fingers get dirty and lips get a little bit greasy, but that's OK. It's all washed down with a local IPA (India Pale Ale) or Aperol Spritz. These brown butter wings crisp up perfectly and don't require any frying. They are baked, which makes for way less guilt and easier clean up too!

Serves 4

Preheat the oven to 425°F (220°C) with the rack in the middle. Spray a baking sheet with cooking spray.

In a saucepan, melt the butter over medium heat. Stir in the garlic. Continue to cook the mixture until it bubbles and brown flecks appear. Swirl the pan occasionally. When the butter has a nutty aroma, transfer it to a bowl so it stops cooking. Stir in the smoked paprika.

Rinse and pat dry the chicken wings. Sprinkle with salt and pepper on both sides.

Bake the chicken for 30 minutes, then flip with a pair of tongs. Cook for another 30 minutes.

Remove the chicken from the oven and toss to coat with the brown butter mixture. Top with fresh herbs. Serve immediately.

# Cowboy Steak Tacos with Quick Pickled Red Onions

## Quick pickled onions

1 medium red onion, sliced into ¼-inch (6-mm) half-moons

¾ cup (180 ml) light-colored vinegar such as white, apple cider or rice

1 clove garlic, smashed

½ tsp sugar

½ tsp salt

½ tsp peppercorns

## Steak

1 lb (450 g) sirloin steak or New York strip

¼ cup (60 ml) canola or vegetable oil

4 cloves garlic, smashed

2 tbsp (30 ml) fresh lime juice

1 tbsp (12 g) chopped fresh cilantro

1 tbsp (15 ml) rice vinegar

1 tsp smoked paprika

1 tsp sugar

½ tsp crushed red pepper flakes

1 tbsp (15 ml) canola or vegetable oil

## Serving

4 small, soft flour or corn tortillas

2 cups (140 g) chopped romaine lettuce

Freshly chopped cilantro

Fresh lime wedges

Freshly sliced jalapeños

Avocado

Cojita cheese

Cowboys have ruled the Wild West for hundreds of years, and their cuisine is a favorite in mountain towns, especially those in Colorado, Utah, Wyoming and Montana. There's no question that cowboys know how to prepare a steak. From taverns to huts to fine restaurants, you will often find a version of steak tacos on the menu. My citrus marinade combined with quick pickled onions is a recipe any cowboy or cowgirl would swing their lasso for!

*Serves 4*

To make the pickled onions, bring 3 cups (700 ml) of water to a boil. Place the sliced onion in a strainer in the sink. In a glass jar or bowl combine the vinegar, garlic, sugar, salt and peppercorns. Mix well until the sugar dissolves. Slowly pour the boiling water over the onion to blanch it just a bit. Place the blanched onion in the bowl with the pickling mixture. Make sure it is coated well. Cover and place in the fridge for at least 30 minutes. These will be delicious for up to a week, so it's great to prepare ahead of time.

To make the steak, combine the oil, garlic, lime juice, cilantro, vinegar, paprika, sugar and red pepper flakes in a glass or nonreactive bowl; mix well. Place the steak in the bowl and make sure it's coated well with the marinade. Cover and marinate in the fridge for at least 1 hour to overnight.

Remove the steak from the marinade and let the excess drip off. Heat a 10-inch (25-cm) cast-iron skillet with the oil over medium-high heat. When the oil is shimmering add the steak. Cook for a few minutes on each side until browned and cooked to your liking. Cooking time also depends on how thick your steak is. When done cooking, cut into ¼-inch (6-mm) slices.

To serve the tacos, place some lettuce in the center of a tortilla. Top with the steak, pickled onions, cilantro and any other toppings you like.

# Rustic Chipotle Spiced Elk Chili

2 tbsp (30 ml) olive oil

1 yellow onion, finely chopped

4 cloves garlic, minced

1 lb (450 g) ground elk

1 zucchini, cut into small pieces

1 (28-oz [795-g]) can petite diced tomatoes

1 (15-oz [425-g]) can tomato sauce

1 (15-oz [425-g]) can black beans, drained and rinsed

1 (15-oz [425-g]) can pinto beans, drained and rinsed

4 chipotle peppers in adobo sauce, minced (adjust to taste)

2 tbsp (30 ml) adobo sauce (adjust to taste)

1 tbsp (6 g) cumin powder

1 tbsp (8 g) chili powder

Salt and pepper to taste

Freshly chopped cilantro

Sour cream

Grated cheddar cheese

Fresh lime wedges

There's nothing like a hearty bowl of chili on a cold fall or winter day. It warms you from the inside out. This chili is bursting with flavor and is by far one of the best I've ever had. The chipotle adds a delicious rustic smoky twist. Every bite will make you feel like you are tucked into a cozy mountain cabin hideaway.

*Serves 4–6*

Heat the oil in a large Dutch oven over medium heat. Add the onion and garlic, and cook about 5 minutes until softened and fragrant. Add the elk and cook for about 6 minutes, or until the elk is browned. Stir often and break up the meat with a wooden spoon. Add the zucchini and cook another 3 minutes, until the zucchini starts to soften.

Pour in the diced tomatoes with their juices, tomato sauce, beans, chipotle peppers, adobo sauce, cumin, chili powder and salt and pepper. Stir well to combine. Taste the chili and make any seasoning and spice adjustments. Simmer the chili, covered, for 1 hour. Serve in bowls topped with cilantro, sour cream, cheese and lime wedges.

Note: *If you are not familiar with the heat of chipotle peppers in adobo, try a small amount first, then add more to taste.*

# Alpine Desserts

With all the extra calories you burn in the mountains, there is always plenty of room for treats. These desserts all have their own sweet charm. Fruits, pastry and chocolate take center stage no matter where you are in the world. All of these sweets are ideally served with your favorite piping-hot mug of coffee or tea. In the Alps it's common to find yourself enjoying a strudel in a pine-walled stube, with the fire roaring and grappa flowing.

# Apfelsplaten (Fried Apple Rings)

*2 large eggs*

*6 tbsp (90 ml) whole milk*

*2 tsp (10 ml) granulated sugar*

*⅛ tsp salt*

*⅛ tsp ground cinnamon*

*¾ cup (93 g) all-purpose flour*

*Peanut oil or any neutral-tasting oil for frying (you can also use ghee for a more buttery flavor)*

*2 apples, peeled, cored and sliced into rings*

*Powdered sugar and cinnamon for dusting*

These fried apple rings are an Austrian favorite. They only take minutes to prepare and are delicious for a not-too-sweet dessert, breakfast or brunch. Be sure to use firm apples such as Granny Smith in this recipe so they hold their shape and don't become mushy.

*Serves 2–4*

Whisk together the eggs, milk, granulated sugar, salt and cinnamon. Stir in the flour until you have a thick yet smooth batter.

Place a layer of paper towels on a sheet pan. Have it handy next to your skillet.

Heat a thin layer of oil over medium-low heat in a 10-inch (25-cm) cast-iron skillet (or a large frying pan).

Dip the apple rings in the batter one at a time, letting the excess batter run off. Fry the rings for about 2 minutes each side until golden brown. Cover the skillet while they cook so the apples soften. Remove with a pair of tongs.

Plate the Apfelsplaten and top with a dusting of powdered sugar and more cinnamon if you like.

# Austrian Apple Strudel

## Strudel dough

2½ cups (312 g) unbleached
all-purpose flour

3 tbsp (45 ml) canola oil or melted
unsalted butter

10–13 tbsp (150–195 ml) cold water
(depends on how dry the air is)

¼ tsp salt

Vegetable oil to coat dough

½ cup (45 g) panko bread crumbs

½ cup (50 g) chopped pecans

## Filling

2 lb (900 g) apples (I prefer a tart,
dense apple like Honeycrisp)

2 tbsp (30 ml) fresh lemon juice

1 tsp ground cinnamon

¼ tsp salt

¾ cup (150 g) light brown sugar,
packed

2 tbsp (30 g) unsalted, melted butter

4 tbsp (60 g) unsalted butter, melted,
for brushing the dough

Powdered sugar for topping

I'll never forget the first strudel cave I visited: a fire-lit room with ancient stone walls dedicated to everything strudel. It was a heavenly haven in the Italian Dolomites in the subterranean level of a beautiful boutique hotel, situated in the predominantly German-speaking Tyrolean village called Fiè allo Sciliar. Austria shares a border with Italy in an Italian province, the South Tyrol. So, even though you are in Italy, the cuisine is reminiscent of its German and Austrian neighbors. Apple strudel is a must-have when you are in an alpine hut or, in my case, a strudel cave at the hotel Romantik Hotel Turm.

*Serves 8*

To make the strudel dough, add the flour and make a well in the center in a large deep bowl or clean work surface. Add the oil, half of the water, and the salt. Start to combine with clean hands. The dough will begin to clump together, and after a minute or so you will be able to knead the dough. Add more water by the tablespoon (15 ml) just until the dough clumps and all the flour can be kneaded in. Continue to knead for 5 minutes until you have a cohesive, stretchy dough ball with no flaky bits. Alternatively, you can add the ingredients to the bowl of a stand mixer and knead with the dough hook for 5 minutes.

Coat the dough ball with some oil and place in a bowl and cover. Leave out at room temperature for 1 hour. This is the stage where the dough will form the gluten network it needs so you can stretch it.

Over medium heat, toast the panko and pecans separately in a dry cast-iron skillet for about 5 to 8 minutes or until they start to brown, mixing often. No need to wash the pan in between ingredients. Watch carefully as each will burn easily once they start to toast.

To roll and shape the dough, start by rolling the dough on a clean, lightly floured work surface. At this point you want to roll it as large as you can, working to get a rectangle at least 10 x 12 inches (25 x 30 cm). If the dough starts to stick, add more flour to the rolling pin and surface.

(continued)

Place a clean, large, white dish towel on a large work surface and lightly flour it. The cloth should be at least 24 x 30 inches (61 x 76 cm) with the horizontal side closest to you. You need fabric that is lint free and light so nothing transfers to the dough.

Next, carefully pick up the dough with your hands and, making loose fists, continue to stretch the dough from the middle out until it is virtually thin enough to see through. Use fingers to gently stretch the dough while your fists do the same. The goal is for the dough to be an even thickness all around. Its final size should be roughly 16 x 24 inches (41 x 61 cm). If you accidentally poke holes that's ok, once the strudel is rolled you won't see them. Gently place the dough back on the cloth. Trim off any thick edges with a knife.

To make the apple filling, core the apples and chop them into ¼-inch (6-mm) pieces. Immediately toss with lemon juice, cinnamon, salt, brown sugar, pecans and melted butter. If the apple mixture sits a while it will form liquid. Be sure to strain them before using.

Preheat the oven to 425°F (220°C) with the rack in the middle.

Immediately brush the dough with the melted butter, leaving 1 tablespoon (15 ml) aside for the top.

Sprinkle on the toasted panko, leaving about a 1-inch (2.5-cm) gap from the edges. Scoop the apples out with a slotted spoon, in case of extra juices. Place the apple mixture across the bottom length of the rectangle leaving about 3 inches (8 cm) from the edge. Start to roll the dough starting from the bottom using the fabric to help keep the dough in place. It acts as a sling so you don't have to touch the very thin, delicate dough. Continue to roll using the cloth to hold things together. About halfway, start to tuck in the edges like a big burrito. Once the strudel is rolled, carefully transfer it over to a piece of parchment, then gently over to a baking tray. If it's too long for the tray, bend it to form a slight crescent shape.

Brush with the remainder of the melted butter. Bake for 20 minutes. Reduce the heat to 350°F (175°C) and continue to bake for another 10 minutes or until the strudel is golden brown.

Let cool a few minutes; dust with powdered sugar, slice and serve. Strudel will keep for 2 to 3 days loosely covered in the fridge. You can serve with vanilla ice cream, homemade whipped cream or crème anglaise.

# Engadin Nut Tart (Nusstorte)

Shortbread crust

¾ cup (6 oz [175 g]) unsalted butter, softened

⅔ cup (75 g) caster sugar

¼ tsp salt

Zest of 1 lemon

1 egg plus 1 extra, whisked for egg wash

2 cups (250 g) unbleached, all-purpose flour, divided

Caramel-walnut filling

⅔ cup (75 g) caster sugar (see notes)

⅓ cup (80 ml) water

¾ cup (200 ml) pouring cream

1½ cups (190 g) walnuts, coarsely chopped

1 tbsp (21 g) honey

¼ tsp salt

One of my favorite things about St. Moritz, Switzerland (besides everything!), is biting into an Engadin Nut Tart. St. Moritz is the largest village in the Engadin valley, where this tart originated. My first experience with this treat was at the five-star hotel Badrutt's Palace. This hotel is iconic, and the tart just as much. The Engadin valley holds tight to their traditions. This tart is an essential if you visit, but not to worry if you haven't already booked your trip. Now you can make it on your own.

*Serves 6*

To make the shortbread crust, combine the butter, sugar, salt, lemon zest and egg in the bowl of a stand mixer. Mix on low, then medium speed with the paddle attachment until well combined. Add the flour in two additions, starting on low and increasing to medium speed. Scrape down the sides and paddle as needed.

Place the dough on a lightly floured work surface. Pat into a disk. Cover in plastic wrap and refrigerate for at least 30 minutes; the dough must be chilled before you roll it out.

To make the filling, place the sugar and water in a stainless steel saucepan over medium heat.

Bring to a boil without stirring until all the sugar is dissolved and the mixture turns light brown. If crystals form on the edges of the pan, brush down the sides of the pan with a wet pastry brush.

Remove from the heat and carefully pour in the cream; be careful as it can splatter. Mix in the walnuts. Place back on low heat and continue to cook and mix for about 3 to 4 minutes until you have a mid-brown, caramel color. Remove from the heat and stir in the honey and salt. Let this cool completely before filling the tart.

Preheat the oven to 350°F (175°C), with the rack in the middle. Spray a 7¾ x 1-inch (20 x 2.5-cm) round tart pan with a removable bottom with cooking spray.

(continued)

Roll out two-thirds of the dough, until it's a bit larger than the tart pan. Gently move the dough onto the pan and press into the edges and the bottom. With a fork, pierce some holes into the bottom of the dough for venting. Keep in fridge until ready to use.

Roll out the rest of the dough to fit just larger than the top of the tart pan. Pour the filling into the tart pan. Spread it evenly around the pan. Wet the edges of the dough already in the tart pan.

Place the dough over the top. Gently press the edges with a fork to seal.

Place the tart pan onto a baking sheet, this will avoid a mess in your oven. Pierce holes on the top with a fork. Brush the dough with the egg wash. Bake for 50 to 55 minutes. Let cool a few minutes before serving.

Notes: *Caster sugar is a very fine sugar. You can either find it at your local market or make it yourself. All you need to do is pulse granulated sugar in your blender or food processor for a few seconds.*

*This dough can be made ahead and frozen. Prepare, wrap tightly in plastic wrap, then in a zip-top bag. Remove from the freezer at least an hour before use. It can be frozen up to 3 months. Use within 3 to 5 days if refrigerating.*

# Base Camp Brown Butter Chocolate Chunk Cookies

1 cup (227 g) unsalted butter

2¼ cups (281 g) unbleached all-purpose flour

1 tsp baking soda

½ tsp salt

1 cup (200 g) light brown sugar, packed

½ cup (100 g) granulated sugar

1 large egg plus 1 egg yolk

2 tsp (30 ml) pure vanilla extract

½ cup (88 g) coarsely chopped semisweet chocolate

½ cup (88 g) coarsely chopped milk chocolate

At the base of Beaver Creek mountain, something very special happens for après-ski. After a long day on the slopes, you are welcomed back to the base by the world-famous Cookie Time Chefs. Both kids and adults anticipate this delicious time of the day. The Chefs carry trays with mountains of freshly baked chocolate chip cookies. How do they select which cookie recipe is the one? Each year BC holds a contest open to the public. They choose five finalists, and the public votes on which cookie will be the Official Chocolate Chip Cookie Recipe of Beaver Creek for that ski season. I will definitely submit this recipe!

*Makes 24 cookies*

---

In a metal saucepan (you want something with a light-colored bottom so you can see the color of the butter), heat the butter over medium heat until it starts to bubble, crackle and foam, about 5 minutes. Swirl the pan often. Continue to cook until the crackling stops and you see browned bits and smell a nutty aroma, about 1 more minute. Transfer the butter with all the browned bits to a bowl and let cool to the touch, about 10 to 15 minutes.

In a bowl, whisk together the flour, baking soda and salt. In a stand mixer with the paddle attachment, combine the melted butter, both sugars, egg, egg yolk and vanilla. Beat until smooth and well combined, about 1 minute. Slowly add the dry mixture and beat on low speed until just combined. Fold in all the chocolate chunks.

Transfer the cookie dough to a clean work surface. Pat into a disk and wrap in plastic wrap.

Chill the cookie dough for at least 1 hour to overnight. Take it out of the refrigerator 25 minutes before you want to bake the cookies. This dough is super firm and will need some time to soften back up.

While the dough is sitting, preheat the oven to 350°F (180°C) with the racks in the upper third of the oven. Prepare two baking sheets with parchment paper.

Place 2 tablespoons of dough in a ball on the cookie sheet, placing each cookie 2 inches (5 cm) apart. Bake for 12 to 15 minutes or until they are golden brown. Let the cookies cool for 10 minutes, then transfer to racks to cool completely.

# Basler Leckerli
# (Swiss Gingerbread Biscuits)

Cookies

¾ cup (250 g) honey

1¼ cups (250 g) granulated sugar

1 tsp ground cinnamon

1 pinch ground cloves

1 pinch ground ginger

1 pinch ground nutmeg

Zest of 1 lemon

2 large eggs

1 tsp pure vanilla extract

¾ cup (100 g) blanched slivered almonds, chopped small

¼ cup (50 g) candied orange peel, chopped small

¼ cup (50 g) candied lemon peel, chopped small

¼ cup (50 g) crystallized ginger, chopped small

2 tbsp (30 ml) Kirsch or brandy

4 cups (500 g) all-purpose flour

1 tbsp (13 g) baking powder

Glaze

½ cup (120 ml) water

1½ cups plus 2 tbsp (200 g) powdered sugar

Topping

⅓ cup (72 g) chopped crystallized ginger

⅓ cup (43 g) chopped, blanched almonds

These biscuits are welcoming after a big day outdoors, they are also the perfect midday snack at the office. Serve with hot tea or coffee. These are wonderful milk dunkers, if you are into that kind of thing! These biscuits will infuse your house with the beautiful fragrance of baked spiced cookies. They are especially delicious during the winter holidays. You can add or subtract the citrus and ginger as you wish.

*Makes 24–48 cookies depending on how thick you roll them*

To make the cookies, combine the honey, granulated sugar, spices and lemon zest in a small saucepan over medium-low heat. Cook until the sugar is melted, about 2 minutes, stirring occasionally. Let this mixture cool. Mix in the eggs, vanilla, almonds, candied citrus, ginger and Kirsch. In another bowl, whisk together the flour and baking powder.

In a large bowl, add the flour mixture to the honey mixture in three additions. This is a very thick dough. Place it onto a work surface covered in plastic wrap. Knead the dough to combine with your hands. Wrap tightly and place in the refrigerator for at least 1 hour to overnight.

Preheat the oven to 350°F (175°C). Prepare a sheet pan with parchment paper.

Place the dough on your work surface between two sheets of wax or parchment paper.

Roll to ½ to ¼ inch (1 cm to 6 mm) thick. This dough will take muscle and will need lots of patience. Do the best you can with the rolling. Trim the sides so you have clean edges. Transfer to the baking sheet. Score the biscuits in the shape and size you want with a knife.

Bake for 12 to 18 minutes; bake time depends on how thick you rolled the dough.

While the biscuits are baking make the glaze. Combine the water and powdered sugar in a saucepan. Bring to a boil, then simmer for about 15 minutes. The glaze will be thick at this point. Don't let it cool as it will harden immediately.

When the biscuits are done baking, pour on the glaze and spread with a brush or soft spatula. Immediately top with the ginger and almonds. Cut the biscuits again on your score lines. Let the biscuits cool before serving.

# Furtaies (Funnel Cakes)

1 cup (250 ml) milk

1½ cups (187 g) unbleached all-purpose flour

3 large eggs, separated

3 tbsp (43 g) unsalted melted butter

2 tbsp (30 ml) grappa, acquavite or schnapps

Pinch of salt

Vegetable or peanut oil for frying

Powdered sugar

Tart fruit jam such as bilberry, cranberry, red currant or sour cherry

Think of this as a chic alpine funnel cake, something that you might happen to indulge in on the South Tyrol, on the slopes of the Alta Badia in the Italian Dolomites. It's covered in powdered sugar—reminiscent of what's blanketing the beautiful pistes that surround you and the deep powder we all dream about! There are many names for this dessert; another you will hear when in that region is strauben. Typically, these funnel cakes are served with a side of tart bilberry jam, which tastes like cranberries.

*Serves 4*

Pour the milk into a large bowl. Gradually stir in the flour with a whisk, making sure there are no lumps in the batter. Add in the egg yolks, butter, grappa and salt. With a hand or stand mixer, whisk the egg whites until stiff peaks form. Fold the whipped egg whites into the batter.

Have a paper towel–lined plate handy. In a pot with high edges, heat 2 inches (5 cm) of oil until it reaches 340°F (171°C). Pour some of the batter into a funnel, sealing off the bottom with your finger. Remove your finger and carefully let the batter drip into the hot oil, starting from the center and working outwards, trying to make the pieces connect.

Fry for 2 to 3 minutes until golden brown, then carefully flip with two spatulas. Cook another 2 minutes. Transfer the furtaies to the paper towels to drain. Continue to cook the rest of the dough. Pile onto the plate.

Dust with powdered sugar and serve immediately with jam on the side.

# Kaiserschmarrn
# (Thick Pancake with Plum Sauce)

### Pancake

1¼ cups (156 g) all-purpose flour

¼ cup (50 g) granulated sugar

¼ tsp salt

3 large eggs

½ cup (120 ml) milk

½ cup (120 ml) heavy cream

Unsalted butter

Powdered sugar for topping

### Plum sauce

½ cup (100 g) granulated sugar

½ cup (120 ml) water

1½ lb (680 g) red plums, pitted and cut into 1-inch (2.5-cm) pieces

½ tsp pure vanilla extract

1 tbsp (15 ml) lemon juice

I always giggle when my backcountry ski buddies dive into a plate of these thick, hot crepes. I first learned about this recipe on the slopes of Davos, Switzerland. We had to duck inside before an off-piste ski hike to wait out a storm. Thankfully we did so I could try this treat!

This broken, sweet and dense pancake is typically served as dessert in Austria, Switzerland and the Tyrol. It's just as delicious served as breakfast or a brunch feast. Traditionally, kaiserschmarrn is served with a plum sauce. You can use any seasonal fruits you have on hand to make a compote—peaches, blueberries, raspberries or strawberries. This sauce is also great over oatmeal, ice cream or yogurt.

*Serves 8*

To make the pancake, sift together the flour, granulated sugar and salt in a bowl. Beat the eggs, milk and cream in the bowl of a stand mixer with the whisk attachment. Beat a few minutes until frothy. Change to the beater attachment and mix in the flour mixture until you have a smooth batter.

Melt a pat of butter in a 10-inch (25-cm) cast-iron skillet over medium heat. Pour some batter in to cover the bottom of the pan. Swirl the batter around so the bottom of the skillet is well coated. Once the batter starts to brown underneath, about 5 minutes, take a spatula and roughly chop up the pancake. Add more batter into the pan. Repeat the same process until you are done cooking all of the batter. At this point you will have a roughly chopped pancake.

To make the plum sauce, combine the granulated sugar and water in a small saucepan. Bring to a boil until the sugar is dissolved, about 3 minutes. Add the plums, vanilla extract and lemon juice, bringing back to a boil. Reduce the heat, simmering the plums with a lid on the pan until they are saucy and tender, about 10 minutes. The sauce will thicken as it cools.

Top the pancakes with the plum sauce and powdered sugar before serving.

# No-Churn Mountain Pine
# Ice Cream

Pine simple syrup

1 cup (25 g) spruce or Douglas pine
needles (no pesticides)

1 cup (200 g) sugar

1 cup (240 ml) water

Ice cream

½ cup (120 ml) pine simple syrup

1 (12-oz [366-ml]) can evaporated milk

2 tsp (10 ml) pure vanilla extract

Pinch of salt

2 cups (473 ml) cold heavy cream

Taste the cool, fresh, breezy scent of mountain pine in this easy to prepare no-churn ice cream. Prepare for holiday parties or steamy summer nights when you are craving a frozen treat. No ice cream machine is necessary, which means you can have homemade ice cream at the ready with way less fuss!

*Serves 6–8*

To make the syrup, rinse the pine needles and chop finely in a food processor. Place the sugar and water in a saucepan. Bring to a boil, whisking until the sugar has dissolved, about 1 minute. Remove the syrup from the heat, and stir in the pine needles. Let the needles soak for at least 3 hours. Strain the syrup into a bowl and discard the pine needles.

To make the ice cream, combine the pine syrup with the evaporated milk, vanilla and salt in a bowl. If the pine syrup is no longer pourable, you can heat it for about 30 seconds in the microwave until it's liquid again. Whip the heavy cream in a stand mixture until stiff peaks form. Fold in the milk mixture. Pour the ice cream batter into a 9-inch (23-cm) loaf pan. Cover with plastic wrap and chill for at least 6 hours, until firm.

# Rustic Blueberry Tart with Pine Nut Crumble Topping

### Dough

1½ cups (187 g) unbleached all-purpose flour

3 tbsp (42 g) granulated sugar

¼ tsp fine salt

10 tbsp (284 g) cold unsalted butter, cut into ¼-inch (6-mm) pieces

5–7 tbsp (75–105 ml) ice water

### Blueberry filling

¼ cup (50 g) granulated sugar

1 tbsp (8 g) cornstarch

1 tsp lemon zest (from ½ medium lemon)

¼ tsp ground ginger

⅛ tsp fine salt

2 cups (12 oz [280 g]) fresh blueberries (do not use frozen)

2 tsp (10 ml) freshly squeezed lemon juice

### Pine nut crumble

¼ cup (31 g) unbleached all-purpose flour

¼ cup (135 g) toasted pine nuts

¼ cup (50 g) light brown sugar, packed

¼ cup (23 g) old-fashioned rolled oats

¼ tsp ground ginger

Pinch of fine salt

¼ cup (57 g) cold unsalted butter, cut into ¼-inch (6-mm) pieces

I got the inspiration for this tart at Dunton Hot Springs, a ghost town from the 1800s located near Telluride, Colorado that's been reborn as a chic, rustic high country resort. Serve this tart with a piping-hot cup of coffee and a cozy wool blanket.

*Serves 4–6*

To make the dough, add the flour, granulated sugar and salt to the bowl of a food processor. Pulse until combined. Add the butter, and pulse until just combined. Add the water, pulsing until the dough just starts to pull together. You can test the dough by pinching it with your fingers. It should come together easily. Turn out the dough onto a work surface and knead it until it's well combined. It will be very crumbly at first, but then it will come together nicely. Pat into a disk and refrigerate for at least 30 minutes to overnight.

To make the filling, combine all of the ingredients for the filling in a bowl.

To make the crumble, combine all of the ingredients for the crumble in another bowl. Press the butter into the rest of the ingredients until clumps form. Chill for at least 30 minutes.

Preheat the oven to 400°F (205°C) with the rack in the middle.

Remove the dough from the refrigerator, place on a lightly floured 14-inch (36-cm) piece of parchment paper, roll the dough until you have a 12-inch (30-cm) round. Add flour as needed to the dough so it doesn't stick.

Place the blueberry filling in the middle, leaving about 2 inches (5 cm) free on the edges. Fold the dough so there's a ½-inch (1.3-cm) gap from the blueberries, crimping every few inches until you have a closed circle. Pinch in any holes should they occur. Gently press the blueberries so they lay slightly flattened. Move the tart onto a baking sheet and refrigerate for 30 minutes. Remove from the refrigerator, and add the cold crumble to the top. Transfer the tart to a room-temperature baking sheet and bake for 30 to 35 minutes; the edges of the crust should be golden brown.

Let the tart cool on the baking sheet a bit. Transfer the tart on the parchment paper to a cooling rack until ready to serve. Discard the parchment before serving.

# Austrian Linzer Tart Cookies

*3 cups (375 g) unbleached all-purpose flour*

*1 cup (96 g) almond flour*

*1 tsp ground cinnamon*

*1 tsp baking powder*

*1 tsp kosher salt*

*1½ cups (340 g) unsalted butter*

*1¼ cups (250 g) granulated sugar*

*2 large eggs*

*1 tsp pure vanilla extract*

*1 cup (230 g) raspberry, fig, tart cherry, lingonberry or cranberry jam*

*Powdered sugar for dusting the tops of the cookies*

I remember falling madly and deeply in love with buttery linzer tart cookies as a kid. Whenever I see them in a bakery case I order a dozen, but I have to admit I like my homemade ones the best! You can use any jam flavor you like best, I love raspberry, tart cherry and cranberry. In these cookies, I use my homemade Fig Jam that you can find on page 98 (see also Alps Cheese and Charcuterie Board, page 96). Make sure to dust with plenty of powdered sugar "snow" to resemble the beautiful mountain pistes!

*Makes about 30 cookies*

---

In a bowl whisk together the flour, almond flour, cinnamon, baking powder and salt.

In the bowl of a stand mixer, with the paddle attachment, combine the butter and granulated sugar on medium-high speed. Mix for a few minutes until well combined and pale in color, scraping down the sides when necessary. Add in the eggs one at a time; mix again until well combined. Mix in the vanilla. Turn off the mixer and add in all of the flour mixture, then mix on low speed until it's just incorporated.

Working on a floured work surface, divide the dough into two equal portions. Flatten into 1-inch (2.5-cm)-thick disks. Wrap separately in plastic wrap. Chill the dough in the refrigerator for at least 2 hours up to 5 days.

Remove the dough from the fridge 15 minutes before you are ready to roll it. Roll in between two sheets of parchment paper to ⅛ to ¼ inch (3 to 6 mm) thick. If the dough cracks, just press it back together. If the dough gets too sticky, you can add more flour to it as you roll. You can also place it back in the refrigerator for 10 minutes to firm back up.

Preheat the oven to 325°F (165°C) with the rack in the middle. Cut shapes from the dough with a 2½-inch (6-cm) cookie cutter (I love hearts for these), cutting an equal amount of tops and bottoms. Cut a hole in the middle of the tops. Carefully move the cookies with a spatula to parchment-lined baking sheets. When all the dough is rolled out and cut, place in the refrigerator for 5 to 10 minutes. Remove from the fridge and bake the cookies for 10 to 12 minutes; they should be lightly golden brown on the edges. Let the cookies cool on the baking sheet for 5 minutes before transferring them to cooling racks.

Dust the tops of the cookies with powdered sugar. Spread the bottoms with some jam. Make cookie sandwiches and serve.

# Campfire Skillet S'mores Dip

2 tbsp (28 g) unsalted butter

9 oz (255 g) milk chocolate chips

9 oz (255 g) semisweet chocolate chips

⅓ cup (78 ml) heavy cream

1 (10-oz [280-g]) bag large or 3 cups (160 g) small marshmallows

16–20 sheets graham crackers

Thankfully, s'mores are a dessert staple in the high country. They are served up in so many creative ways. What could be more fabulous (and simple to prepare) than roasted marshmallows and chocolate? My skillet dip version is a favorite when feeding a crowd. It's perfect for camping and alpine-themed snacking. Watch how big your guests smile when this melty skillet is served.

*Serves 8–10*

Preheat the oven to 400°F (205°C).

Place the butter in a 10-inch (25-cm) cast-iron skillet and melt the butter in the oven. Remove the skillet from the oven and add the chocolate chips, drizzling the cream over the top. Decorate the top with the marshmallows. Heat in the oven for 5 to 6 minutes or until the marshmallows are golden brown.

Serve immediately with the graham crackers for dipping.

# Sacher Torte

## Cake

6 oz (170 g) bittersweet chocolate, cut into small pieces (use at least 50% cacao)

6 tbsp (85 g) unsalted butter

4 egg yolks

4 oz (114 g) powdered sugar, divided

5 egg whites

¼ tsp salt

⅓ cup (42 g) pastry flour

## Filling

½ cup (150 g) apricot preserves

1 tbsp (15 ml) dark rum

## Glaze

6 oz (170 g) bittersweet chocolate, cut into small pieces

2 tbsp (28 g) unsalted butter

¼ cup (60 ml) heavy cream

Enjoying a food pit stop on the trail is always fun and delicious. It's especially important when a storm rolls in; sometimes it's too cold or the visibility is too dangerous to keep moving. This Viennese chocolate torte served with a piping-hot cup of espresso can make the coldest outdoors enthusiasts warm again. Versions of this torte are served in both the finest five-star restaurants and rustic alpine huts. It's a blissful treat for chocolate lovers.

*Serves 8*

Preheat the oven to 350°F (175°C). Prepare a 9 x 2-inch (23 x 5-cm) cake pan with butter and flour.

To make the cake, melt the chocolate and butter over a double boiler. Set aside to cool. In a mixer with the whisk attachment, whisk the egg yolks with 1 ounce (28 g) of the powdered sugar until light, creamy and pale. Beat the chocolate into this mixture until well combined. Transfer to another large bowl.

Clean the mixer bowl well. Add the egg whites and salt. Whisk until you have soft peaks. Add the remaining 3 ounces (86 g) of powdered sugar, and continue to whisk until you have stiff peaks. Fold in the flour.

Gently fold one-third of the egg whites into the chocolate mixture. This will lighten it. Continue to fold in the egg whites gently until you have a smooth, light batter. Pour the batter into the prepared cake pan. Bake for 40 minutes, or until a thin knife stuck into the center of the cake comes out dry. Cool the cake on a rack completely before cutting. When cake is cool, place on a piece of parchment paper.

To make the filling, puree the apricot preserves with the rum. Slice the cake in half. Spread the apricot filling evenly over the cake. Top with the second layer.

To make the glaze, melt the chocolate and butter over a double boiler. Bring the cream to a boil. Stir in the melted chocolate until well combined. Pour the glaze over the top of the cake, nudge it down the sides and gently smooth with an offset spatula. Let the cake cool for 30 minutes before serving. Gently transfer the cake to a cake plate with the help of two spatulas.

# Lavender Goat Cheese Truffles

*⅓ cup (80 ml) heavy cream*

*1 tbsp (8 g) dried lavender buds*

*4 oz (114 g) goat cheese*

*2 tbsp (43 g) honey*

*½ tsp pure vanilla extract*

*6 oz (170 g) melted semisweet chocolate, 60%–70% cocoa*

*Unsweetened cocoa powder for rolling truffles*

Chocolate lovers you will swoon over this exotic blend of flavors. Alpine goat cheese adds a creaminess and gourmet twist to rich chocolate truffles. The lavender essence is calming and fragrant. We have a fundraising cooking competition here in my mountain town called the Telluride Top Chef and Taste of Telluride. It's a fun, social event in which we can taste samples from all of our restaurants in town. Local chefs try to outdo each other with morsels of savories, sweets and cocktails. My favorite bite was by our local cheese and charcuterie shop called Over the Moon. Their version of these was to die for . . . so I just had to make my own to share with you!

*Makes 20 truffles*

---

In a saucepan, bring the cream to a simmer, be careful not to boil. Remove from the heat and pour into a bowl. Stir in the lavender. Let steep for 10 minutes so the lavender infuses into the cream. Place a fine mesh sieve over another bowl. Strain the cream into the bowl, mashing the lavender into the bottom of the sieve to release all the flavor. In another bowl, combine the cream, goat cheese, honey and vanilla extract.

Melt the chocolate over a double boiler or bain marie. Fold the melted chocolate into the cheese mixture. Combine well. Chill in the refrigerator for 1 hour.

Using a small melon baller or teaspoon, scoop out portions of the truffle mix. Roll truffle balls with clean hands. Continue to roll until you have used up all the mix.

Place some cocoa powder into a bowl. Toss the truffles in the cocoa powder. Chill again on a cookie sheet until ready to serve. Store, covered airtight in the fridge up to 5 days.

# Bourbon Peach Semifreddo

### Bourbon roasted peaches

3 or 4 ripe peaches

¼ cup (60 ml) pure maple syrup

2 tbsp (28 g) unsalted butter, melted

¼ cup (60 ml) bourbon

### Semifreddo

1½ cups (360 ml) chilled heavy cream

4 large eggs, separated

1 tsp bourbon

½ tsp pure vanilla extract

⅔ cup (133 g) sugar, divided

1 cup (225 g) bourbon roasted peaches (see above)

One of the best parts about summer here in the mountains is biting into a juicy, ripe Palisade peach. These beauties are bursting with flavor and beg to be enjoyed in so many ways. If your peaches get too ripe to eat out of hand, then this frozen, refreshing semifreddo is a great way to enjoy them.

*Serves 8*

To make the peaches, preheat the oven to 375°F (190°C). Cut the peaches in half and discard the pits. Place the peaches cut sides up in a baking dish with 3 tablespoons of (45 ml) water in the bottom of the dish. In a small bowl, combine the maple syrup, butter and bourbon. Pour this mixture evenly over the peaches. Bake for 35 to 40 minutes or until the peaches are soft and just about to lose their shape. Remove from the oven and let the peaches cool. Now you can easily remove the skins from the peaches. Chop the peaches into small pieces. Set aside.

To make the semifreddo, spray a 9 x 5-inch (23 x 13-cm) loaf pan with cooking spray. Line it with plastic wrap, draping the extra off the sides of the pan. Smooth out the plastic wrap as much as you can with your hands.

In the bowl of a stand mixer, using the whisk attachment, whip the cold cream, starting on low, then increase to medium speed. Whip until soft peaks form. Transfer to a bowl and chill.

Clean the bowl and whisk attachment. Add the egg yolks, vanilla, bourbon and ⅓ cup (67 g) of the sugar. Mix on high speed until pale and fluffy, about 3 minutes. Transfer to a large mixing bowl and set aside.

Clean the bowl and whisk attachment one final time. Add the egg whites and mix on medium speed until they get frothy, about 1 minute. Increase the speed to high and slowly pour in the remaining ⅓ cup (67 g) of sugar. Beat until you have stiff peaks, about 4 minutes.

Fold the chilled whipped cream into the egg yolk mixture with a soft silicone spatula. Using the same spatula, gently fold a third of the egg whites into the yolk mix. Fold in another third, then the peaches, then the last third. Incorporate all well, but try not to deflate the batter.

Spoon the batter into the lined loaf pan. Evenly spread it with an offset spatula. Cover with more plastic wrap, smoothing out the wrinkles and bubbles with your hands as you go. Freeze until firm, at least 8 hours, but overnight is best.

To serve, you can use an ice cream scoop straight out of the pan or you can invert the semifreddo onto a serving dish and cut into slices. Let it warm for 10 to 15 minutes on a counter so it slides out easily.

# Luscious Libations

There's always a reason to raise a glass in the mountains. Toasting to the natural beauty is essential, and saying cheers with dear friends is the best. You might be warming up fireside after a frosty day on the slopes, or may be cooling down after catching a prize-winning trout in the heat of the summer. After epic mountain bike rides thirst needs to be quenched. I told you, there is always a reason to raise a glass in the mountains! Cheers!

# Alpenglow Martini

## Rhubarb sauce

3 cups (710 ml) water

1½ cups (300 g) sugar

5 stalks rhubarb (700 g), washed and chopped into 1-inch (2.5-cm) pieces

1 tbsp (15 ml) fresh lemon juice

## Martini

Lemon zest for bottom of glass

2 oz (60 ml) gin

2 oz (56 g) rhubarb sauce

1 oz (30 ml) fresh lemon juice

Ice

This cocktail is reminiscent of the brilliant pink glow we see reflected on the mountains at sunset. The alpenglow in the mountains becomes almost a religious experience, and it's not to be missed. Catch it when you can as it's gone in just minutes, similar to this cocktail! It's made with a homemade rhubarb sauce and gin. This sauce is also great on pancakes and yogurt parfaits. If you cannot get your hands on rhubarb, this cocktail is equally as fabulous with strawberries or raspberries.

*Makes 1 martini and 3 cups (700 g) rhubarb sauce (enough for 12 cocktails!)*

To make the rhubarb sauce, combine the water and sugar, bringing it to a boil over high heat in a saucepan. Stir to help the sugar dissolve. Add the rhubarb and simmer for 5 to 10 minutes, until the rhubarb starts to soften. Mash the rhubarb against the side of the pan with the back of a spoon. Stir in the lemon juice. The sauce will thicken as it cooks and as it cools. Transfer to a blender and purée until well combined.

To make the martini, place a slice of lemon zest on the bottom of the chilled martini glass. Combine all of the ingredients in an ice-filled cocktail shaker. Strain into the glass.

# Strawberry Lemon Gingerade

¼ cup (60 ml) water

2 cups (400 g) fresh strawberries, cleaned and remove tops

2 tbsp (16 g) minced fresh ginger

⅓–½ cup (67–100 g) sugar (depends on your sweet tooth)

½ cup (120 ml) fresh lemon juice (about 2 large lemons)

25 oz (750 ml) sparkling water

Lemon wedges for serving

Living at high altitude means it's very necessary to stay well hydrated at all times. The thin air up here makes you super breathy and very thirsty even doing the most minimal of activity. This lemonade is thirst quenching and very delicious. My kids love when this drink is waiting for them after a long day hiking the trails. Adults can create a boozy twist with this cooling drink too—for each glass, you add an ounce or two of vodka, rum or tequila.

*Serves 6*

In a saucepan, bring the water, strawberries, ginger and sugar to a boil. Cover the pot and simmer for 10 minutes or until the strawberries are very soft and releasing all of their juices.

Place a fine-mesh sieve over a deep bowl. Pour the strawberry mixture into the sieve. Mash the mixture with a spatula onto the bottom of the sieve to release all of the juices. Continue until all of the juices are in the bowl. Discard the pulp. The juice you are left with is now a simple syrup.

Pour the lemon juice into the strawberry-ginger simple syrup. Mix to combine.

Pour the strawberry syrup into a large pitcher. Top with the sparkling water. Top with lots of ice.

Serve in ice-filled glasses with a lemon wedge.

# Wiener Eiskaffee
# (Viennese Iced Coffee)

*2 scoops (69 g) vanilla ice cream*

*½–1 cup (120–240 ml) strong brewed coffee*

*Whipped cream (about ¼ cup [60 ml] per serving)*

*Unsweetened cocoa powder or chocolate shavings for serving*

This decadent iced coffee is the perfect treat after a long hike or fishing trip. The perfect combo of ice cream and coffee. Pillows of whipped cream always add fun to any flavor adventure. Enjoy this cafe favorite in the comfort of your own home. A great treat for parties too . . . you can make minis for after dinner sweet tooth cravings. If you are craving a boozy twist, feel free to add a shot of rum, vodka or the spirit of your choice.

*Serves 1*

Place the ice cream in a chilled glass. Pour the coffee over it. Top with whipped cream and cocoa powder.

Note: *For homemade whipped cream, pour 1 cup (235 ml) of chilled heavy cream into the bowl of a stand mixer. With the whisk attachment, whisk on low speed until the cream starts to thicken. Increase the speed to medium until soft peaks start to form. Add your favorite sweetener to taste, starting with 1 tablespoon (12 g) and adding from there. I like powdered sugar or maple syrup. Increase the mixer speed to high until you have stiff peaks. Use immediately or store in an airtight container until ready to use.*

# Schümli Pflümli
# (Sweetened Coffee with Plum Schnapps)

*1 tsp sugar (or sweeten to taste)*
*1½ oz (45 ml) plum liqueur*
*5 oz (150 ml) strong brewed coffee*
*Slightly sweetened whipped cream*
*Dusting of cocoa powder*

You can find this cocktail in ski huts around the Swiss Alps. I first enjoyed this hot, boozy drink in a warming hut on the slopes of Davos, Switzerland. We were waiting out a winter storm and my ski guide, Keni, encouraged me to give this a whirl. I immediately fell in love with the Schümli Pflümli. I love it both for its silly name and combination of ingredients. It really does warm you up on a cold winter's day!

*Serves 1*

Heat a stem glass with some hot water and pour it out. Add the sugar and liqueur to the glass. Fill the glass with the coffee and stir all together. Top with the whipped cream and dusting of cocoa powder.

# The Polar Queen Cocktail

**Simple syrup**

1 cup (240 ml) water

1 cup (200 g) sugar


Ice

3 oz (90 ml) half-and-half

1½ oz (45 ml) silver tequila

1 oz (30 ml) peppermint schnapps
(such as Rumplemintz)

2 tsp (10 ml) simple syrup

Peppermint stick dust

Mini candy canes

I love naming cocktails after favorite ski runs. Polar Queen is the name of one of our blue intermediate runs in Telluride. It's a gentle piste and super fun for warming up the legs. Speaking of warming up, this minty cocktail will do just that.

*Serves 1*

To make the simple syrup, in a saucepan, bring the water and sugar to a boil over medium-high heat. Stir until the sugar is dissolved. Transfer to a jar to cool. Store sealed in the refrigerator until ready to use.

Fill a cocktail shaker with some ice. Add all of the ingredients except the crushed peppermint stick and mini candy cane and shake well. Pour through a strainer. Top with crushed peppermint stick dust and a mini candy cane.

# Nutty Nord Cocktail

Brown sugar for rim of glass

Ice

3 oz (90 ml) Nocello liqueur (walnut flavored)

1½ oz (45 ml) heavy cream

Pinch of ground nutmeg

Pinch of ground cinnamon

A Nord is a person from the North who lives for the snow—someone who relishes in all activities that revolve around the winter, especially all forms of Nordic skiing. I have plenty of Nord friends, and they have taught me a whole lot about the alpine world. As a matter of fact, I do consider myself a tried and true Nord too. This drink is a toast to them and all of us who could live forever inside a snow globe. Cheers to the Sons and Daughters of the Snow . . .

*Serves 1*

Rim a coupe glass with brown sugar. In an ice-filled cocktail shaker add the Nocello, cream, nutmeg and cinnamon. Shake well. Pour into the coupe glass. Top with a sprinkle of cinnamon.

Serve immediately.

# Raspberry Fire Cocktail

Handful fresh raspberries

Ice

Coarse salt for glass

1½ oz (45 ml) silver or reposado tequila

1 tbsp (15 ml) freshly squeezed lime juice (½ lime)

1 tbsp (15 g) agave (or to taste)

1 tsp raspberry jam

Pinch of cayenne pepper, optional

When the temps warm up or cool down, this Telluride favorite (mixology inspired by our local Thai hot spot, Siam) will fire you up with a blend of tequila, fresh lime, smashed raspberries and a spoonful of raspberry jam for a little extra sweetness. Want to add a little more fire? Throw in a pinch of cayenne pepper to your cocktail shaker. Think of it as a margarita en fuego!

Serves 1

Muddle the raspberries in a small bowl with the back of a spoon. Rim a chilled old-fashioned glass with salt. Pour the muddled raspberries into the salted glass. Top with some ice.

In an ice-filled cocktail shaker add the tequila, lime juice, agave and raspberry jam (add cayenne if you wish). Shake well until combined. Strain into the old-fashioned glass. Top with some fresh raspberries.

# The Chairlift Warmer Cocktail

1½ oz (44 g) semisweet or dark chocolate

1 tbsp (6 g) cocoa powder

2 tbsp (28 g) sugar (or to taste)

1 cup (240 ml) 2% milk, divided

Salt

2 oz (60 ml) peppermint schnapps

Shot of espresso, optional

Whipped cream

Sprinkles

Peppermint stick

Cozying up with a warming cocktail is one of life's greatest pleasures. In winter, the temps can be frigid—but it's still super fun to play outdoors. To warm things up, it can become essential to pop into a warming hut. I've been in tents, chalets and yurts around the world; a constant is they have some version of spiked hot chocolate. Taking a few sips of this warms you from the inside out. When you head back out to ski or snowshoe you will feel just a little bit toastier.

Serves 1

In a small saucepan, whisk together the chocolate, cocoa and sugar in half of the milk. Once it's combined, whisk in the rest of the milk and a pinch of salt. Pour into a thermal container or mug. Stir in the schnapps. If adding espresso, do so now.

Top with whipped cream, sprinkles and a peppermint stick.

Note: *Use the most high-quality chocolate and cocoa powder you can find. It will really amplify the flavor.*

# Grappa Sour

2 oz (60 ml) grappa

Juice from ½ fresh lemon

Juice from ½ fresh lime

1 chilled egg white

Splash of St-Germain (elderflower liqueur)

Splash of simple syrup (see page 161)

Dash of Angostura or orange-flavored bitters

I'll never forget my first time in an underground grappa cave in the South Tyrol, tucked in a tiny village in the Italian Dolomites. They had so much grappa and the party scene was going off. There were many varieties and let's just say I tried quite a few of them. This Grappa Sour really highlights this fragrant (high-octane) brandy!

Serves 1

Shake all of the ingredients except for the bitters well in a cocktail shaker with no ice. Strain into a chilled coupe glass. Top with a few drops of the bitters.

# Loaded Bloody Mary

Ice

Juice from ½ lemon

Juice from ½ lime

6 oz (180 ml) tomato juice

2 oz (60 ml) vodka

2 tsp (10 g) prepared horseradish

1 tsp Tabasco (or more if you crave spicy)

1 tsp Worcestershire sauce

Pinch of smoked paprika

Pinch of black pepper

Pinch of sea salt

### Garnishes

1 Rancher's Bison Slider (page 110)

Pickled onions

Cornichons

Stuffed olives with pimento

Cooked bacon slices

1 celery rib

The Bloody Mary cocktail is a brunch staple in many different locations around the globe, but here in the mountains we go *big*—larger than life and oversized. Our Bloodys are often a full meal. Make a statement at your next brunch and serve this loaded and unforgettable cocktail. My Bloody Mary is not shy and will be the hit at any gathering. Perched on top is one of my Rancher's Bison Sliders (page 110). You will also need skewers or get creative with tent pegs.

*Serves 1*

Fill a chilled highball glass with ice and set aside.

Squeeze the lemon and lime wedges into a cocktail shaker and drop them in. Add the remaining mix ingredients and fill the shaker with ice. Shake gently and strain into the ice-filled glass. Garnish with the listed ingredients. Don't be shy here—the sky's the limit!

# Crushed Blackberry Bourbon Mountain Mule

*Handful of fresh blackberries*
*1 tbsp (15 ml) fresh lime juice*
*1½ oz (45 ml) bourbon*
*6 oz (180 ml) chilled ginger beer*
*Ice cubes*
*Lime wedge, fresh mint and blackberries for garnish*

Whether for a summer cooler or a winter warmer, ripe blackberries, bourbon and ginger beer will give you that mountain kick after a long day. This cocktail is sunny, sparkling and just a bit oaky from the bourbon. You'll feel the corners of your mouth flip up as soon as you take a taste.

*Serves 1*

Muddle the blackberries and lime juice with a wooden spoon on the bottom of a chilled copper mule mug. Pour in the bourbon and ginger beer. Stir to combine. Add the ice. Top with lime wedges, mint and blackberries.

# Cranberry Glögg

2 (750-ml) bottles dry red wine

1 (750-ml) bottle sweet red wine, such as muscatel (or moscato)

1 lemon

1 orange

10 anise pods

5 cardamom pods

5 cloves

3 cinnamon sticks

1 inch (2.5 cm) fresh ginger, thinly sliced

1 cup (150 g) raisins

1 cup (125 g) toasted walnuts

1 cup (200 g) sugar (or to taste)

1 tbsp (15 ml) bitters

1 cup (250 ml) brandy

Craving a very traditional winter beverage? Glögg is the answer. This is a sweet mulled wine, and the recipes for it are as diverse as the regions that serve it. The building blocks are red wine, brandy, spices, nuts and fruits. It's served hot and the fun that happens surrounding it is unforgettable. Whether you are après-skiing or après–snow shoveling, a delicious glass of glögg will warm you right up.

*Serves 12*

Combine the wines in a large enameled or stainless-steel soup pot. Zest the citrus fruits. Squeeze the juices of the fruits into the wine. Tie up the lemon peel, orange peel and spices in a cheesecloth and add to the wine. Add the raisins, walnuts and sugar.

Bring the wine mixture to a boil. Reduce heat and gently simmer for 15 minutes. Cook until the flavors are blended and the walnuts are soft. Skim occasionally to remove any foam. Add sugar to taste and any other seasonings you like to taste more of.

Just before serving, add the bitters and brandy. Ladle the glögg into glass mugs or warmed, tall stemmed glasses. If serving in stemware, make sure the glögg is not piping hot. Serve with spoons for eating the raisins and walnuts.

# Acknowledgments

Writing a book is a journey—a delicious, creative one that takes a team of amazing people to honor the project from concept to completion.

Big thanks to all those who believed in me and helped me conquer one of my biggest life goals. I am beyond thrilled to share my favorite high alpine recipes with you in print.

Hugs to all the readers and fans of MarlaMeridith.com: You inspire me every single day to do the job I LOVE to do!

This cookbook journey started with an email inquiry from Page Street Publishing. Next came some fun brainstorming sessions and then a green light. Huge thanks to the entire team over there. You have all been so professional, organized and stellar with communication every single step of the way.

Donna Benner, you are a great light in my life. Thank you for believing in me and helping me share the MM brand with the world. Looking forward to future endeavors together.

Lindsay Andreotti, your wisdom, insight and brilliant understanding of human potential got me from a single Post-It® note to writing an entire book. You are a total rock star. Please continue to work with people the way you do and you will change the world for the better.

My beautiful kids (Leela and Lucas) and dear friends in Telluride: You were awesome and inspiring recipe testers. It was fun feeding you!

Moose and Bo (my coonhounds): You did a great job cleaning up after me in the kitchen.

To all the professional chefs I've met along the way, who have taught me so very much about alpine cuisine and cooking in general. Thank you for graciously inviting me into your kitchens and restaurants and treating me to such beautiful food and drink! Thank you also to the wonderful guides, travel companies and hotel partners I've had the pleasure of working with around the world. I look forward to connecting with you all again some day soon.

Mom and Dad, without you none of this would have happened. Thanks for your love, support and constantly being my biggest fans.

Namaste,

Marla

# About the Author

Marla Meridith is a celebrity food and lifestyle blogger at MarlaMeridith.com and an online influencer with over 1 million fans across her social platforms, which have garnered attention from loyal readers around the world. She is the photographer, stylist and recipe developer for her visually rich blog. She lives in Telluride, Colorado, with her two children and two hound dogs.

# Index